D1605989

Writing 39

Robert Creeley

Was That a Real Poem
& other essays

With a Chronology by Mary Novik

Edited by Donald Allen

Four Seasons Foundation
Bolinas, California

Library of Congress Cataloging in Publication Data:

Creeley, Robert, 1926–
    Was that a real poem & other essays.

    (Writing series: 39)
    I. Allen, Donald Merriam, 1912–   II. Title.
PS3505.R43W36   814'.5'4   78-16254
ISBN 0-87704-041-9
ISBN 0-87704-042-7 pbk.

ACKNOWLEDGMENTS

Grateful acknowledgment is made to the original publishers of these essays:

The *Times Literary Supplement* for "A Sense of Measure," published August 6, 1964.

AMS Press, Inc., for the Introduction to their reprint of *Black Mountain Review,* 1969.

Penguin Books Ltd. for the Introduction to *Whitman Selected by Robert Creeley,* Poet to Poet Series, 1973.

John Martin and Black Sparrow Press for "The Creative," published as *Sparrow* 6 in March 1973. (Originally given as a lecture entitled "Creativity: The Moving Force of Society?" as part of the Milton S. Eisenhower Symposium, at Johns Hopkins University, 1972.)

For "Inside Out," published as *Sparrow* 14, November 1973. (Originally given as a lecture as part of the Buffalo Conference on Autobiography in the Independent American Cinema at the Center for Media Study, the State University of New York at Buffalo, on March 23, 1973.)

For "Was That a Real Poem or Did You Just Make It up Yourself," published as *Sparrow* 40 in January 1976; and in *American Poets in 1976,* edited by William Heyen (Indianapolis: Bobbs-Merrill Co., Inc., 1976).

And for the Introduction to Charles Reznikoff's *The Manner "Music,"* 1977.

Yves Le Pellec for "Last Night" published in *Entretiens* 34, 1975.

Margins for "For Michael," published in No. 18, March 1975.

Neil A. Chassman and the Dallas Museum of Fine Arts for "On the Road," published in the catalog of the exhibition *Poets of the Cities, New York and San Francisco 1950-1965* (New York: E. P. Dutton & Co., Inc., 1974).

"Here" was commissioned by Leon Amiel, publisher, for a projected volume (1979) of Robert Indiana's designs for Gertrude Stein's *The Mother of Us All.*

"Three Films" is the text of a lecture given for the Rocky Mountain Film Center, University of Colorado, Boulder, June 22, 1978.

Douglas Calhoun for "A Creeley Chronology" by Mary Novik, published in *Athanor* No.4, Spring 1973.

CONTENTS

Preface

The notes and essays here assembled argue no progress *ad Parnassum*, as Pound might say, and presuming that *essay* has something to do with old-fashioned Christian trying, that's what each factually was: an attempt to get something said. I might add, as well, that all but two were written for payment—which recalls a lovely answer Ed Dorn once gave some snoop who wanted to know why he didn't write "for money," to which he answered: "Everything I write is for money. It's just that no one wants to pay." For years I was terrified of being compromised by any intimation of depending on writing for a living. But now I just want to sit in the street and scream, "Goddamnit, *pay* me!" Or read on, whichever is simpler.

More aptly, how *is* one to make the case for such a hero as Whitman, or R.B. Kitaj, inveterate fellow American who has finally won *that* old war by virtue of the fact he'll paint the murals for the new entrance to the British Museum, using Eliot's *The Waste Land* for subject—terrific!—or "The Creative," or literal poems did prove the constant of a life? I could sit down and try it all again.

Although these pieces are a random coherence, so to

speak, I am certainly the common denominator and pleased to accept that responsibility. My only regret is that I can't now talk on and on, but must admit, in common with all, the accuracy of Pound's Law of Discourse: say what you have to say, and then shut up. . . . But the ambiguity of that *have* still invites.

R.C.
Placitas, N.M.
May 15, 1978

Was That a Real Poem
& other essays

A Sense of Measure

I am wary of any didactic program for the arts and yet I cannot ignore the fact that poetry, in my own terms of experience, obtains to an unequivocal order. What I deny, then, is any assumption that that order can be either acknowledged or gained by intellectual assertion, or will, or some like intention to shape language to a purpose which the literal act of writing does not itself discover. Such senses of pattern as I would admit are those having to do with a preparatory ritual, and however vague it may sound, I mean simply that character of invocation common to both prayer and children's games.

But it is more relevant here to make understood that I do not feel the usual sense of *subject* in poetry to be of much use. My generation has a particular qualification to make of this factor because it came of age at a time when a man's writing was either admitted or denied in point of its agreement with the then fashionable concerns of 'poetic' comment. William Carlos Williams was, in this way, as much criticized for the things he said as for the way in which he said them. I feel that 'subject' is at best a material of the poem, and that poems finally derive from some deeper complex of activity.

I am interested, for example, to find that "automatic or inspirational speech tends everywhere to fall into metrical patterns" as E.R. Dodds notes in *The Greeks and the Irrational*. Blake's "Hear the voice of the Bard" demands realization of a human phenomenon, not recognition of some social type. If we think of the orders of experience commonly now acknowledged, and of the incidence of what we call *chance*, it must be seen that no merely intellectual program can find reality, much less admit it, in a world so complexly various as ours has proved.

Recent studies in this country involved with defining the so-called creative personality have defined very little indeed and yet one of their proposals interests me. It is that men and women engaged in the arts have a much higher tolerance for disorder than is the usual case. This means, to me, that poets among others involved in comparable acts have an intuitive apprehension of a coherence which permits them a much greater admission of the real, the phenomenal world, than those otherwise placed can allow. Perhaps this is little more than what Otto Rank said some time ago in *Art and Artist* concerning the fact that an artist does die with each thing he does, in so far as he depends upon the conclusion of what possibilities do exist for him. Paradoxically, nothing can follow from that which is altogether successful. But again this risk is overcome—in the imagination—by trust of that coherence which no other means can discover. It would seem to me that occasional parallels between the arts and religion may well come from this coincidence of attitude, at least at times when philosophy or psychology are not the measure of either.

Lest I be misunderstood—by 'religion' I mean a basic *visionary* experience, not a social order or commitment, still less a moral one. Gary Snyder tells me that the Indians consider the experience of visions a requisite for attaining manhood. So they felt their enemy, the whites, not men, simply that so few of the latter had ever gained this measure of their own phenomenality. In this sense I am more interested, at present, in what is *given* to me to write apart from what I might intend. I have never explicitly known—before writing—what it was that I would say. For myself, articulation is the intelligent ability to recognize the experience of what is so given, in words. I do not feel that such a sense of writing is 'mindless' or 'automatic' in a pejorative way. At the end of *Paterson V* Williams writes:

—learning with age to sleep my life away:
saying .

The measure intervenes, to measure is all we know . . .

I am deeply interested in the act of such *measure*, and I feel it to involve much more than an academic sense of metric. There can no longer be a significant discussion of the meter of a poem in relation to iambs and like terms because linguistics has offered a much more detailed and sensitive register of this part of a poem's activity. Nor do I feel measure to involve the humanistic attempt to relate all phenomena to the scale of human appreciation thereof. And systems of language—the world of discourse which so contained Sartre et al.—are also for me a false situation if it is assumed they offer a modality for being, apart from description. I am not at all interested in describing anything.

I want to give witness not to the thought of myself—that specious concept of identity—but, rather, to what I am as simple agency, a thing evidently alive by virtue of such activity. I want, as Charles Olson says, to come into the world. Measure, then, is my testament. What uses me is what I use and in that complex measure is the issue. I cannot cut down trees with my bare hand, which is measure of both tree and hand. In that way I feel that poetry, in the very subtlety of its relation to image and rhythm, offers an intensely various record of such facts. It is equally one of them.

Black Mountain Review

In hindsight it is almost too simple to note the reasons for the publication of the *Black Mountain Review*. Toward the end of 1953 Black Mountain College—a decisive experimental school started in the early thirties by John Rice and others in Black Mountain, North Carolina—was trying to solve a persistent and most awkward problem. In order to survive it needed a much larger student enrollment, and the usual bulletins and announcements of summer programs seemed to have little effect. Either they failed to reach people who might well prove interested, or else the nature of the college itself was so little known that no one quite trusted its proposals. In consequence a summer workshop in pottery, which had among its faculty Hamada, Bernard Leach, and Peter Voulkos, found itself with some six rather dazzled persons for students. Whatever the cause—and no doubt it involves too the fact that all experimental colleges faced a very marked apathy during the fifties—some other means of finding and interesting prospective students had to be managed, and so it was that Charles Olson, then rector of the college, proposed to the other faculty members that a magazine might prove a more active advertisement for the nature and form of the college's program than the kind of announcement they had been depending upon.

This, at least, is a brief sense of how the college itself came to be involved in the funding of the magazine's publication. The costs, if I remember rightly, were about $500 an issue, so that the budget for a year's publication would be about $2000—hardly a large figure. But the college was in such tight financial condition that it could not easily find any money for any purpose, and so its support of the magazine, most accurately the decision of the faculty to commit such an amount to that purpose, is a deeply generous and characteristic act. Too, it's to be acknowledged that Olson's powers of persuasion were considerable.

The nature of the magazine itself, however, and the actual means of its publication, that is, literally its printing, are of another story which is really quite separate from the college itself. In the late forties, while living in Littleton, N.H., I had tried to start a magazine with the help of a college friend, Jacob Leed. He was living in Lititz, Pennsylvania, and had an old George Washington handpress. It was on that that we proposed to print the magazine. Then, at an unhappily critical moment, he broke his arm, I came running from New Hampshire—but after a full day's labor we found we had set two pages only, each with a single poem. So that was that.

What then to do with the material we had collected? Thanks to the occasion, I had found excuse to write to both Ezra Pound and William Carlos Williams. I didn't know what I really wanted of them but was of course deeply honored that they took me in any sense seriously. Pound very quickly seized on the possibility of our magazine's becoming in some sense a *feeder* for his own commitments, but was clearly a little questioning of our *modus operandi.* What he did give me, with quick generosity and clarity, was a kind of *rule book* for the editing of any magazine. For example, he suggested I think of the magazine as a center around which, "not a box within which/ any item." He proposed that verse consisted of a constant and a variant, and then told me to think from that to the context of a magazine. He suggested I get at least four others, on whom I could depend unequivocally for material, and to make their work the mainstay of the magazine's form. But then, he said, let the rest of it, roughly half, be as various and hogwild as possible, "so that any idiot thinks he has a chance of getting in." He cited instances of what he considered effective editing, *The Little Review* and the *Nouvelle Revue Française* when its editor gave complete license to the nucleus of writers on whom he depended 'to write freely what they chose.' Williams in like sense gave us active support and tried to put us in touch with other young writers, as Pound also did, who might help us find a company. But with our failure to find a means to print the magazine, it all came to an abrupt end. I remember Pound's consoling me with the comment that perhaps it was wise for "the Creel" to wait for a while before "he highflyz as editor," but things seemed bleak indeed.

Happily, there was what proved to be a very significant alternative. Cid Corman, then living in Boston and having also a weekly radio program there called *"This Is Poetry,"* had come to be a friend. I had heard the program, by some fluke, in New Hampshire, wrote him, was not long after invited by him to read on the program, and soon after we were corresponding frequently, much involved with senses of contemporary writers and writing. It was Cid, in fact, who got me in touch with Olson, by way of their mutual friend, Vincent Ferrini—who sent me some of Olson's poems, with his own, for possible use in the magazine that had not yet collapsed. In returning Olson's poems to Vincent, I made the somewhat glib remark that he seemed to be "looking for a language," and got thereby my first letter from Olson himself, not particularly pleased by my comment and wanting to discuss it further, like they say. The letters thus resulting were really my education just that their range and articulation took me into terms of writing and many other areas indeed which I otherwise might never have entered. But the point now is that Cid, once Jake Leed's and my magazine was clearly dead, undertook himself to publish a magazine called *Origin*. Significantly enough, its first issue includes some of the material I had collected—for example, Paul Blackburn's, whom I had come to know through Pound's agency—and features the work of Charles Olson, specifically the first of the *Maximus* sequence as well as other poems and prose.

Origin was, in fact, the meeting place for many of the writers who subsequently became the active nucleus for the *Black Mountain Review*. More than any other magazine of that period, it undertook to make place for the particular poets who later come to be called the "Black Mountain School." In its issues prior to 1954, and continuingly, it gave first significant American publication to Denise Levertov, Irving Layton, Robert Duncan, Paul Carroll, Paul Blackburn, Larry Eigner, myself and a number of others as well. Although I had, for example, published stories in the *Kenyon Review* and the *New Directions Annual*, neither place could afford me the actual company nor the range of my own work that *Origin's* second issue provided. For me it was an acknowledgement I had almost begun to think impossible, and I am sure that Cid's consistent support of our writing has much to do with what became of it.

The point is that we felt, all of us, a great distance from the more conventional magazines of that time. Either they were dominated by the New Critics, with whom we could have no relation, or else they were so general in character, that no active center of coherence was possible. There were exceptions certainly. *Golden Goose*, edited by Frederick Eckman and Richard Wirtz Emerson, was clearly partisan to myself and also to Olson, and published my first book, *Le Fou*, and would have published a collection of Olson's, *The Praises*, but for a misunderstanding between him and the editors, when the book was already in proof. Both men were much involved with Williams, and made

his example and commitment the center for their own.
There were also other, more occasional magazines, as *Goad*
—whose editor, Horace Schwartz, involved me in a useful
defense of my interest in Ezra Pound, just that it helped
clarify my own terms of value.

But, with the exception of *Origin*, and possibly *Golden Goose* also, only two magazines of that time, the early
fifties, had finally either the occasion or the sense of pro-
cedure, which served as my own measure of the possibility.
One, *Fragmente*, edited and published in Freiberg, Germany,
by Rainer Gerhardt—whose acquaintance I was also to make
through Pound's help—was an heroically ambitious attempt
to bring back into the German literary canon all that writing which the years of the Third Reich had absented from
it. Rainer and his wife, living in great poverty with two
young sons, were nonetheless able to introduce to the German context an incredible range of work, including that of
Olson, Williams, Pound, Bunting, and myself. I was its American editor but its literal activity was completely the ef-
forts of Rainer and Renate. Their conception of what such
a magazine *might* accomplish was a deep lesson to me. They
saw the possibility of *changing* the context of writing, and
I think myself that this magazine, and also the small paper-
backs they were able to publish, effectually accomplished
this for present German poetry—despite the bitter fact of
Rainer's early death.

In like sense, a group of young writers of various na-
tionalities centered in Paris was of great interest to me.
They were led by a lovely, obdurate and resourceful Scot,
Alexander Trocchi, and included the British poet, Chris-
topher Logue, and the brilliant American translator, Aust-
ryn Wainhouse. Others too were of equal interest, Patrick
Bowles, for example, who translated the first of Beckett's
French novels into English—and Richard Seaver, who was
later to become a decisive editor for Grove Press. Again,
what these men proposed to do with their magazine, *Merlin*, and the books which they also published with the help

of the Olympia Press as Collection Merlin, was to change
the situation of literary context and evaluation. I've given
a brief, personal sense of my relation to Trocchi in a novel,
The Island, where he figures as "Manus," and I was also invited by them to be an associate editor on the magazine—
but by that time the funds necessary to continue publication of the magazine were not obtainable. But their translation of Genet and Beckett's work as well as their brilliant
critical writing, which extended to political thinking as well
as literary, made them an exceptional example of what a
group of writers might do.

By 1954 my wife and I were already much involved
with a small press called the Divers Press. We had moved
from France to Mallorca, and had become close friends
with a young English couple, Martin Seymour-Smith and his
wife, Janet. It was Martin who first interested us in publishing books, since, as he pointed out, printing costs were ex-
ceptionally cheap on the island and so much might be done
on a shoestring. But our initial venture together, the Roebuck Press, came a cropper because Martin's interests were
not really decisively my own nor mine his. We did publish
a selection of his poems, *All Devils Fading*, but our center
was finally in writers like Olson (*Mayan Letters*), Paul
Blackburn (*Proensa* and *The Dissolving Fabric*), Irving Layton (*In the Midst of My Fever*), Douglas Woolf (*The Hypo-
critic Days*), Larry Eigner (*From the Sustaining Air*), and,
though he comes a bit later, Robert Duncan (*Caesar's Gate*).
We also published Katue Kitasono's *Black Rain*, and it is a
design of his that is used for the covers of the first four issues of the *Black Mountain Review* as well as another on
the credits page. What I felt was the purpose of the press
has much to do with my initial sense of the magazine also.
For me, and the other writers who came to be involved, it
was a place defined by our own activity and accomplished
altogether by ourselves—a *place* wherein we might make
evident what we, as writers, had found to be significant,
both for ourselves and for that world—no doubt often

vague to us indeed—we hoped our writing might enter. To be published in the *Kenyon Review* was too much like being "tapped" for a fraternity. It was too often all over before one got there, and few if any of one's own fellow writers came too. Therefore there had to be both a press and a magazine absolutely specific to one's own commitments and possibilities. Nothing short of that was good enough.

Origin had already done, in some sense, as much as one could hope for, and I remember having doubts about either the use of the practicality of simply another magazine more or less "like" it. I certainly didn't want to compete with Cid. But one possibility did seem to me lacking in *Origin*, despite occasional notes and reviews, and that was the *ground* that an active, ranging critical section might effect. I wasn't thinking of criticism finally as judgment of whether or no this or that book might be deemed "good" or "bad." What I hoped for, and happily did get, was critical writing that would break down habits of "subject" and gain a new experience of context generally. If I have any disappointment in the magazine in retrospect, it's only that this part of it does not extend as far as I had hoped. Still, Jung's "The Mass & the Individuation Process" (in the 5th issue)—which I remember he sent to "The Black Mount Review," which pun, unintentional I assume, was a delight—and Borges' "Three Versions of Judas" (in the 7th issue) —which I read with absolute seriousness, not realizing it was a "fiction"—are some instance of what I was after. But, and here I was much influenced by Olson, the possible *range* of such writing as we conceived of it was never fully demonstrated.

There have been various comments and summaries published with respect to the *Black Mountain Review*'s activity as a little magazine. Most lively and helpful, I think, is Paul Blackburn's account which appears in *Kulchur* (Vol. 3, No. 10, Summer 1963), called "The Grinding Down." Among other things, he identifies the initials used by reviewers in the first four issues, and also the pseudonyms used for signature in some other instances. Too, Kent State University Library, in one of its bulletins, provides an accurate and useful bibliography together with a brief note by myself. But now I think it best that the pseudonyms stay pseudonyms, and that initials, if not recognized (I used three sets, for example), be part of the present reader's experience. Often I, or some friend I could quickly get hold of, had to fill blank pages, to manage our length of sixty-four pages, or subsequently the longer format of two hundred and twenty plus. I at times had nightmares of having to write the whole thing myself.

The contributing editors listed in the first issue conform to that sense Pound had earlier made clear: get a center of people you can depend on for consistently active contributions, elsewise you'll have nothing to build with. Olson was to prove that center almost single-handedly, but Blackburn was also very helpful, with all manner of support including legwork around New York to get the magazine into stores as well as much sympathetic and practical handholding. Layton I had come to know through a Canadian mimeographed magazine, *Contact*, which many of us had been involved with as its contents will show. He had an intensive energy and obviously was restless with what was then the Canadian literary milieu. His brother-in-law, John Sutherland, editor of the *Northern Review*, no longer invited him to literary parties because Irving's conduct was too irascible. So he was an unequivocal cohort and wrote, happily, voluminous amounts of verse. If I remember rightly, I also asked others as well—in particular Paul Goodman, who answered he'd prefer being just a contributor, since his other commitments very possibly would not give him time to do more. Rexroth generously agreed although we had little information of each other beyond his own public figure. Less happily, by the time he'd read the first issue, he had realized his error and his withdrawal (as well as that of Paul Blackburn, whose reasons were happily less adamant) is noted at the back of the Fall 1954 issue along with a defensive comment by myself.

Many of the writers who became very decisive to the magazine are not so listed, however. Robert Duncan is very much one of these. His first contribution, sent at Olson's suggestion, was a poem I in turn suggested we print a section of—and Duncan's response was to the effect that if he *had* wanted a section of the poem printed, he *would* have sent it—and I learned much from him also. There was one very amusing confusion involved with a poem of his I did print, in the Fall 1954 issue, "Letters for Denise Levertov: An A Muse Ment." Apparently Denise, for some reason, took it as a parody on her own way of writing, and was thus hurt. And Olson too thought it was some kind of attack on him. I think that poor Duncan and myself were the only ones unequivocally to enjoy it, and it remains for me an extraordinary summary and *exempla* of contemporary possibilities in poetry.

Denise herself, Louis Zukofsky (whom I found thanks to Edward Dahlberg and also Duncan), Jonathan Williams, and Robert Hellman (a close friend first in France, who subsequently came to teach briefly at Black Mountain), all were of great help to me in that they were there to be depended on, for specific writing but equally, for a very real sense of the whole act's not being merely a whistling in the dark but something making a way. God knows one often doubted it. Holding to Pound's sense of letting at least part of the magazine seem wide open, I know I printed work at times that any of them must have been puzzled by. Some things I just liked, for example, Gautier's "The Hippopotamus," which appears in the 5th issue. I still do. However, I've never found anyone to share my pleasure in "The Goat Man" by Harold Lee Drake, in the 6th issue. He wrote, to put it mildly, extraordinary prose—including one piece involved with masturbating by the seashore, which the condition of censorship in the fifties never permitted me to print. He was one of the contributors who came out of nowhere, and unhappily seems to have returned there, since

I've never seen his work printed again.

Of contributors generally, I've defined, I think, the character of one group clearly evident throughout the magazine's publication. These are writers who have either come together earlier, in *Origin*, or who are "found" by the same nature of attention that *Origin*'s preoccupations had effected. Louis Zukofsky would be one of these latter as would be also Edward Dahlberg. There are also "occasional" contributors, as Paul Goodman, and those who simply appear with no previous or necessarily continuing sense of relationship, like James Purdy. I think we were, possibly, the first magazine to print his work in America, and that was surely a pleasure. He had found us somehow, submitted the story, and I printed it. The same is true of Sherry Mangan's story (a curious echo from the twenties) in the 7th issue, or of Alfred Kreymborg's "Metaphysical Ballad" printed there as well.

But two other kinds of contributor were particularly significant. Thus far the relation to the college itself must seem the fact that it was paying for the magazine's publication, and that Olson was the rector of the college. Although Hellman, Duncan, and myself were briefly on the faculty, this was somewhat after the fact because the nature of the magazine was determined otherwise and really prior to that fact. But if those contributors are noted who were either students at the college at the time, or had recently been so, then a relation of the college to the magazine, and particularly to Olson's influence as a teacher, becomes very clear. First there is Jonathan Williams—who is certainly not a "student" at this point, but who is much interested in the college and in Olson particularly, as his own publishing (*Jargon*) makes clear. Look at the advertisements for his press in the various issues of the magazine, for further instance. Then there is Joel Oppenheimer, who had left the college not long before the publication of the first issue and so comes into its activity by that fact. Then Fielding Dawson—also absent at this point from the college, in the army in Stuttgart, but again much involved by relation to the college and so to the magazine also. Then there are those literally there: Edward Dorn, Michael Rumaker, and Tom Field. Dorn had published one poem in *Origin*, in an issue edited by Denise Levertov, and his story in the *Black Mountain Review* is, I think, his first published prose—and clear example of what is to be his extraordinary ability in that mode as well as in poetry. Michael Rumaker has his first publication of any kind in the magazine, with two stories I feel to be as fine as ever were published—in fact, "The Pipe" I think as exceptional a piece of writing as any of any time. Then, finally, Tom Field—actually a painter, but whose writing struck me usefully, though it has not proven of major interest to himself. But think of it—that a college having an enrollment of about *twenty* people as average during the time the magazine is published should have such gifted men as Dorn, Rumaker, Dawson, Oppenheimer, and Williams have so proven themselves to be. Hopefully, it makes excuse for the kind of eulogy these comments must now seem.

The college closed in the spring of 1956 and at that point Jonathan Williams became the ostensible publisher of the last issue—on the cover of which he put a little sticker to make this fact clear. There was hope we might continue. Some material for the next issue was in hand, some photos of Frederick Sommer for one thing, and some essays of Edward Dahlberg's. But the last issue itself was almost impossible to manage. I had left Black Mountain, had been briefly in San Francisco, and was now living in New Mexico. The printer, of course, was still in Spain, and the delays in proofing, or even getting the initial printing begun, were almost impossible to manage. However, the last issue—with the addition of Allen Ginsberg as contributing editor—defines the last group of contributors who have particular relevance. Ed Dorn had moved to San Francisco with his family after leaving Black Mountain the year previous. I was in restless state, having separated from my wife, and being really at odds with much in my life. I wanted a new condition and so went west, where I'd never been, to see if that might be an answer. So I was also in San Francisco, in the spring of 1956—and for a writer there was really no place that could have been quite like it, just at that time. The contents pages of the 7th issue will make this much clearer than I can—Ginsberg, Kerouac, Whalen, McClure, Burroughs (Lee), Snyder—and another man I was deeply pleased to include, albeit from the east, Hubert Selby, Jr. It was unequivocally a shift and opening of the previous center, and finally as good a place as any to end. Other magazines had appeared as well, with much the same concerns, among them *Big Table* and the *Evergreen Review*. Whatever battle had been the case did seem effectually won.

A last note, briefly, about the divers reproductions and photographs that appear in the various issues, as well as the covers for the last three. . . . I valued these especially, in that they freshened everything when otherwise things seemed almost too dense. It was a particular honor to include Franz Kline, Philip Guston, Aaron Siskind, and Harry Callahan, because all had been teachers at the college, and, even more than that, had each made so actively clear a new way of seeing in their art. John Altoon I can never thank enough for so much it would be specious to try to list it— and he also had made very evident how extraordinary a painter he is. Dan Rice, a close friend of those days and first met at the college—the same. Edward Corbett I met while I was editing the last issue in New Mexico, and though I'm sure he thought I was simply hysterical, his cover as well as other generosities is a lovely fact of his concern. As for Laubiès—he saw it all.

So it's finally all well in the past, either as one's own experience of something, or else the communal fact of what the writers of that situation and time seemed to have had in mind. I don't think it can ever be very different. You want to do something, to see it happen, and apparently it can't, or at least can't with what then exists as possibility. So you

try to change it, and you do or don't as proves the case.
What really now delights me is that a magazine having a
usual printing of some five to seven hundred and fifty
copies, about two hundred of which ever got distributed,
could have made any dent whatsoever. That should cheer
us all.

Placitas, N.M.
December 15, 1968

The Creative

"Why wert thou a creature wanting soule?
Or, why is this imortall that thou hast?"
—Marlowe, *Dr. Faustus*

One seems to begin at a beginning, and then, after a time
as difficult to recognize the actual measure of as any other
thing that may or may not happen, one comes to an end.
In that literal situation of what one calls experience, the
outward, call it, of the content of perception, a life is lived
in the explicit package of meat one calls the body. A mind
thinks of it, at first so intrinsically the organism itself that
there is, apparently, no separation experienced. The eyes
see, the mouth tastes, the nose smells, the ears hear, the
hands touch and hold, the legs stretch and walk. Hair, skin,
bone, the body fills, voids, heats, cools, sleeps, wakes. An
interminable one of many, the thought of life apart from
itself is vague, impossible to consider. There is no one but
instantly proves all, *people* some vast horizontal of seemingly similar size, a growth then of precisely repetitive proportions.

I want to speak of *creative* in the simply complex situation of: what creative means to me. Ezra Pound wrote
of the deceptive syntactical simplicity of the request, "Buy
me the kind of Rembrandt I like"—as complex in actuality
as the numbers of people who might make it. Speaking

now, it must be that this factual person, *me*, is familiar, so
like so many, in fact, his hair, teeth, pants, etc. But the *I*,
as Wittgenstein put it, is what is "deeply mysterious." In a
world of objects, *me*s, this is the one manifestation of existence that cannot so see itself as literal *thing*. It is my experience that what I feel to be the creative has location in
this place of personal identity.

A friend recently here told me of a book he'd been
reading wherein the creative as a concept is attributed to
Renaissance art and its artists, although they felt their notion to have in turn roots in their own sense of historical
past. This fact—as it instantly, 'creatively,' became one in
my thinking—coincided with another I had got from Giedion's discussion of *abstraction* in the first volume of *The
Eternal Present*. As he says, "Like the symbol, abstraction
came into being with the beginning of art. It existed: name-
less. It was simply there. . ." Certainly these two agencies,
symbol and abstraction, have a powerful resonance in any
situation we speak of as 'creative,' or surely they have had.
To take from this that, to make another—this must, in
thinking, be an extraordinary act of mind—to have of another a one, itself thus thing of the other, symbolic, and
yet apart, abstract—so becomes the magic we feel in all
transformation. Initially, as Giedion assumes it, there were
two possibilities in abstraction: the ability to make of all
the seemingly endless divergency and occasion of thing a
general agreement, a *one* in which the *all* of its situation
might come to rest and be recognized; but also, the impulse
to have the one be a part of the whole, in a way which
overrode it, became specific more intensely than all the
other 'parts' otherwise equally present, an 'I' that wants
so much more than to be merely 'human' or 'people' or,
simply, 'like them.' Giedion notes that there is an increasing social egocentricity in that time between the Middle
Ages and the Renaissance, although it is myself who calls
it 'social'—a feeling that what the elders of our own time
felt as 'individual sensibility,' an insistence on the intrin-

sic value of what each one of us may feel, think, or value as singular persons, was growing in multiple social senses at this time. Giedion also emphasizes that it is this same dominance of egocentricity that permits Descartes to say, "I think, therefore I am," and to make thus separation of emotion and intellect in the context of human experience. The *abstraction* here accomplished is of the second kind.

We may feel as common persons of the world a terror we will not be given specific witness, that no one will ever know our actual lives have been lived at all. But why, I wonder, do we so imagine our lives *not* to have their own inherent orders, as Charles Olson might say—or why do we so wish to extend ourselves beyond the literal, the usual, even the casual circumstances of any day we do so live? As such persons we yearn for the possibility, as we would say, of doing something truly 'creative,' 'different,' not at all like anything anyone has ever done before. It is as if that sadly insistent 'humanism' of Descartes, that intensely flat and drab *rationalism*, had taken us to pure possibility—We think!—and then left us there to ponder: What can we think of now? Unhappily there is an automatism just as actual in processes of thought as might be felt to be in processes of digestion. My own irritation with the notion of creativity, as it has to do with writing, and, frankly, with living as well, is that it has been so given this place of the will—as though an act of thought resolved as an intention became thereby instanter revelation.

I had hoped, ignorantly, that *create* and *credible* might share some root, thinking of the Spanish *creo (I believe)*—because it would be lovely indeed if creation and belief were joined at some initial point in their experience. However, that is not the case, but 'create' is issue of such lovely company I see no reason to be disappointed: *"ker-.* To grow. Suffixed form **ker-es-* in Latin *Ceres,* goddess of agriculture, especially the growth of fruits," whence our *cereal.* Or in the Latin *creare,* "to cause to grow." Or the O-grade forms in "**kor-wo-,* 'growing,' adolescent, in Greek *kouros,* *koros,* boy, son" and in **kor-wa,* "in Greek *kore,* girl, maiden, pupil of the eye." Or that most lovely, possibly: "Compound *sm-kero-,* 'of one growth' (**sem-,* same, one . .), in Latin *sincerus,* pure, clean": whence our *sincere.* "Only the most absolute sincerity under heaven can effect any change."

One should, after all, have danced more, under the moon, and been a farmer, instead of a man given to thought. At least one has been father and teacher, giving such care as one knew how to, sincerely, to that growth of persons, in places very possibly not the most suitable. One had created them—hearing sometimes as blessing, sometimes as snigger, *fruit of my loins. Fruit of the loom, loam. You fruit. First fruits. The fruit of their labor.* I remember that early *create* meant *make,* for me, insofar as I had apparently created a disturbance, had made a mess. Woodenly, I could see no very clear difference in the fact and stubbornly set out to make a poem, a man, of myself. I thought you could think of it, and, having plans, follow them till the thing appeared, gloriously, complete. In like sense the creation of the world seemed to me a specific labor of God's in the same way this building seems the specific labor of men. My company in this dilemma was obviously a number of my nineteenth-century countrymen, who seem to have made love, money, and monsters, all with the same convictions. One can hear even now, for example, that anguished voice shouting, "I have created a monster!" The possible 'disturbance' was unquestionably the real point in mind.

Our contemporary 'creations' are somewhat drabber: dresses, new styles, sad brittle poems written in sterile surroundings to mechanical senses of the possibility. But why should one be so hostile to what is, after all, a very human hope that something might thus change, might come to be said—*be new?* What does one know of creation except that insistent "Make it new," which Pound so emphasized? But he says also, "I have brought the great ball of crystal; / who can lift it?/ Can you enter the great acorn of light?"

It is possible we live entirely in that act we so call 'creative,' that that is, in fact, the place of our possibility and recognition of life—that that fact of *place* is a mind, that *body* is equally the idea of it which possesses us. I am struck by the situation of schizophrenia wherein the experience of body may so place the hands or feet or anus in the consciousness so affected, that no communal agreement as to their location is possible. A *self-created* reality in that way dominates and isolates the one who has become, even without intention or agreement, its world.

In like sense, one of the human dilemmas of artists, particularly of writers who are participant in a kind of image-making that has as agency that most powerful, possibly, of human abstractions, *language*, is megalomania, delusions of greatness, of exceeding power or omnipotence. There is persistent impatience with those unwilling or unable to enter the world so proposed, and its obviousness to the one who has served as its creator makes him appear *fascistically*, in the political sense, determined upon its actuality and harmonious economy. One can think instantly of a diversity of writers who exhibit that situation in greater or less degree: Knut Hamson, Céline, Wyndham Lewis, D. H. Lawrence, and Ezra Pound himself. The world, so to speak, depends upon them for its own realization, but as they work to accomplish this reality, another world, equally present, insists upon those limits, which they, humanly, must accept.

To say of someone, that their appearance is *pleasant*, or *ugly*—each are creative acts. A 'world' in each case occurs in which that person takes place, whether or no his or her agreement is given. "Give a dog a bad name . . ." is not a specious homily but recognition, however casual, of the power of naming. "A rose by any other name . . ." might well smell as sweet, but not the *rose*—that would no longer exist, and an odor only would be the point. For years I have been intrigued by a quotation of Louis Zukofsky's from Wittgenstein: "A point in space is a [the?] place for an argument . . ." Think of it. Is that the point? What point? What has come to it? Who is present and realizes that to be the case? When? Is there the possibility of agreement in any such situation? "How many angels can dance on the head of a pin?" True questions of a reality experienced as *created*—that is to say, in this case, something said. "I didn't mean to hurt you. I loved, love, will love—you. Here. There. Then. Now." "The indefinite period of time yet to be . . ."

It is that *spell* of words that now comes to mind, and one had forgotten, thinking back all those years, to fusty smells of oiled corridors and boots and wet coats, sitting, trying to think, to remember, how does one spell 'patient' . . . Spelling! So obviously and so simply evident—and the grammar, the *glamour*, is instantly present, the patient 'patient,' and the heavy dead odor of the sickroom, roses in a vase beside the bed, because roses, not dandelions, cost explicit money and betoken care and tender concern. So you do have me 'under your spell,' and it is 'that old black magic,' again.

But quickly that other 'world' I had mentioned asserts itself, demanding time, demanding one be in it, physically *actual*. Robert Duncan, with characteristic clarity, posits the situation of these two 'worlds' as *reality* and *actuality*. The real is what we value in *real* estate, and has to do with things of this life: *res, rei*—possession, thing. *Re*public—dig it . . . One for all and all for one. But the actual has got that 'act' in it: "actus, an ACT." It's moving, causing things to skitter and bump, get on with it in some actual sense. One can return to reality by way of the *actuarial*, having to do with the computing of insurance risks and premiums, etc., etc., but it will never be the same. Which is to say, the tree is real, but when you hit it, it's actual.

"Don't you poets get tired of living in a world of your own imagination and want to get back to reality?" Whose reality? Who owns all this? The Swedish poet Lars Gustafsson pointed out to me that marriage, like the car, is an invention. It is not actual, although for many people indeed it may be real. But one doesn't drink it, nor stumble over it, throw it on the fire. It isn't flesh or fur or fin. You'll remember the story of the sad fisherman who was given three wishes, who was both married and caught in reality, so that the demand upon him was to get more and more of that substance. Things upon things upon things—and no place to be. No one actually home at all, no matter it was all too real. It's an equally sad mistake to think that what is called 'creative' in poetry seeks a bargain in space and time, wants to exchange this for that, hike up the prices, so to speak. When Robert Graves writes, "There is one story, and one story only, that is worth your telling . . . ," he claims for poet that power of *revelation*, that care specific to this gift that the elemental nature of existence *not* be lost in the thought of it.

At the funeral of Jackson Pollock, Wednesday, August 15, 1956, the minister, the Reverend George Nicholson, read from St. Paul's statement, Romans, Chapter 8: "The world of creation cannot as yet see reality, not because it chooses to be blind, but because in God's purpose it has been so limited—yet it has been given hope." Later he said, not really having known Pollock but in a very certain sense cognizant of the occasion: "It seemed to me that at that moment when the art world had collected around that grave, on that beautiful day, all our skills & philosophies added up to a fragmentary & sorry collection. Like Plato's cave we were men living in a shadowy illusory world of sounds & sights—like dogs in an art gallery—sniffing around at corners.

"No, I didn't know J. Pollock. But in the Epistle to the Romans Chapter 8 there is more than a hint of glory and greatness—always in short supply."

Charles Olson's response to 'creative' social thinking was a muted sneer, "Oh, change it altogether . . ."—much like Pound's, "you who think you will/ get through hell in a hurry . . ." The point is: "Who even dead, yet hath his mind entire!/ This sound came in the dark/ First must thou go the road/ to hell . . ." "First came the seen, then thus the palpable/ Elysium, though it were in the halls of hell,/ What thou lovest well is thy true heritage/ What thou lov'st well shall not be reft from thee . . ."

Pound's respect for Confucius, for that "sound given off by the heart's core," the possibility of things said, is measure of the *sincerity* I had earlier invoked. Whitman insisted, "The theme is creative and has vista," and in his sincerity, the heart of the matter, an imagination found the literal body of its impulse realized, made substantive, transformed. For it is *imagination*, only, which has this possibility. Hear it. "Only the imagination is real!/ I have declared it/ time without end . . ." "Light, the imagination/ and love,/ in our age,/ by natural law,/ which we worship,/ maintain/ all of a piece/ their dominance." Realize that you *have been* told, by the myriad men and women for whom *creation* is the literal place we live in, under sky, on ground, by water, in air. Pollock said, "When I am *in* my painting, I am not aware of what I'm doing. It is only after a sort of 'get acquainted' period that I see what I have been about. I have no fears about making changes, destroying the image, etc., because the painting has a life of its own. I try to let it come through. It is only when I lose contact with the painting that the result is a mess. Otherwise there is pure harmony, an easy give and take, and the painting comes out well."

What is here to discover is neither new nor significantly esoteric. Henry Corbin, in the introduction to *Creative Imagination in the Sufism of Ibn 'Arabi*, makes this useful point: "Today, with the help of phenomenology, we are able to examine the way in which man experiences his relationship to the world without reducing the objective data of this experience to data of sense perception or limiting the field of true and meaningful knowledge to the mere operations of the rational understanding. Freed from an old impasse, we have learned to register and to make use of the

36

intentions implicit in all the acts of consciousness or trans-consciousness. To say that the Imagination (or love, or sympathy, or any other sentiment) *induces knowledge*, and knowledge of an 'object' which is proper to it, no longer smacks of paradox." Thus you will recognize the sadly familiar, and *useless*, difficulty William Carlos Williams meets with in "The Desert Music": "You seem quite normal. Can you tell me? Why / does one want to write a poem?// Because it's there to be written.// Oh. A matter of inspiration then?// Of necessity.// Oh. But what sets it off?// I am that he whose brains/ are scattered/ aimlessly . . ." At the close of this extraordinary poem the moment of revelation is literally accomplished: "I *am* a poet! I/ am. I am a poet, I reaffirmed, ashamed// Now the music volleys through as in/ a lonely moment I hear it. Now it is all/ about me. The dance! The verb detaches itself/ seeking to become articulate . . ." The word *dances*, in the literal garden of *desire*.

Louis Zukofsky wrote, "Out of deep need . . ." But what nature of *need* is it? To eat, to sleep, to find a form merely? I question that. In Berlin I am delighted to discover that the eminent scientist Heisenberg, himself in Munich, has fallen upon the arts as though upon a blissful bed of flowers, *knowing*, in his age, as Gregory Corso would say, that the *conceptual* dilemma of the sciences leads them round and around the careful maze of their various *contexts*, true Bottoms but alas no Shakespeares to love them and get them home. Zukofsky also writes of these *things made*, these *poems*, as being source of profound solace—where the heart finds rest. It is the need to *enter* what we loosely call the vision, to be one with the Imago Mundi, that image of the world we each of us carry within us as possibility itself. What can we say otherwise? Peace, brother. It's going to be all right. It's soon over and it won't hurt.

But the heart *aches*—"Out of deep need . . ." Corbin: "This power of the heart is what is especially designated by the word *himma*, a word whose content is perhaps best suggested by the Greek word *enthymesis*, which signifies the act of meditating, conceiving, imagining, projecting, ardently desiring—in other words, of having (something) present in the *thymos*, which is vital force, soul, heart, intention, thought, desire . . . The force of an *intention* so powerful as to project and realize ('essentiate') a being external to the being who conceives the intention, corresponds perfectly to the character of the mysterious power that Ibn 'Arabi designates as *himma* . . . Thanks to his representational faculty . . . every man creates in his Active Imagination things having existence only in this faculty. This is the general rule. But by his *himma* the gnostic *creates* something which exists outside the seat of this faculty . . . In the first case, as it is exercised by most men, its function is representational; it produces images which are merely part of the conjoined Imagination . . . , inseparable from the subject. But even here, pure representation does not, *eo ipso*, mean 'illusion,' these images really 'exist,' illusion occurs when we misunderstand their mode of being. In the case of the gnostic . . . , the Active Imagination serves the *himma* which, by its concentration, is capable of *creating* objects, of producing changes in the outside world . . . When in contemplating an image, an icon, others recognize and perceive as a divine image the vision beheld by the artist who created the image, it is because of the spiritual creativity, the *himma* which the artist put into his work. Here we have a compelling term of comparison, by which to measure the decadence of our dreams and of our arts . . ."

Well, no use no way, *and* comparisons *are* odious—and the plan we had was that all this was going to get it together and be a happy place to be *in*, like. But that *himma* shit, man, that's *really* my kind of people. Heart-felt. I really mean it, this time, this place, this ——. He forgot the word, walking around, was momently in Bolinas, Berlin, Oslo, Bergen, London, Bolinas—time's like that, sometimes. Days spent watching surfers, days spend time like there was no end to it, forever. "He wants impossible liveforever . . ."

"Capsules wherein we wrap up our punishable secrets . . ."
You going to read us a *poem*, Bob? "Who even dead, yet
hath his mind entire!"

You really have to believe in it, as Coleridge said, all
those years ago, so gently, "the willing suspension of disbelief . . ." Like that lovely, 'once upon a time . . .' I knew
a man once who had a lovely team of horses, this was in
West Acton, Mass., and one of them kneeled on a nail was
in the planking of the stall, and the knee got infected—Mr.
Green was his name—and Mr. Green, who lived alone with
his wife, both about in their seventies, he used to, literally,
take the blankets off their bed, this was in winter, and go
out into the stall and wrap up that horse and put poultices
on her knee, to draw out the poison, and he'd sit there
with her, all the night, and finally the old horse, old in its
own way as him, got well.

Take it from there, cut through. Breaks in time, head.
Allen Ginsberg feels poems to be 'time capsules,' messages
you don't really get the fact of till later. Have those bones
begun to sprout—Eliot? True poet, not at all that he wanted
to be—so rational, so Augustan in that old elegance. Let's
create a spectacle! The sixties had 'happenings': "I painted
'I love what I'm doing' in orange and blue. When I got to
'what I'm doing,' it was going very fast, and I picked up
one of the jars and drank the paint, and then I poured the
other two jars of paint over my head, quickly, and dove . . .
through the canvas . . ."

Such report as I had of studies done some years ago
at the University of California at Berkeley, and at Stanford,
of the situation of 'creative' behavior and personality with
respect to specific persons, seemed to indicate a rather low
return of information. Who can be anticipated as being in a
situation with a high potential for creative behavior? No
one apparently, with any surety. One may be born into a
family of ten children, or one, have both parents actively
present, or none, have a high degree of affluence present,
or none, be black, white, yellow, red—without much

proving the case. In like sense specific training in areas deemed creative, as music, dance, art, writing may or may not effect anything. The composer Morton Subotnik pointed out that by far the greater number of eminently competent classical musicians, call them, in this country were the children of Russian Jews, simply that no other group could so unremarkably oblige their children to practice their instrument for six to eight hours daily, from the tender age of three onward. He himself was an exceptional clarinetist and had lovely wish fulfillment dreams in which both his arms were removed from his body, blissfully. He even joined the army, hoping to break the spell—but was instantly put into Special Services, to play the clarinet. Finally, in his early twenties, he managed, of his own will, to put it down. What he had *wanted* to play, aged three, was the trombone, but he could not name it for his parents, and when they showed him endless pictures of musical instruments, in consternation and fatigue he pointed to the clarinet as being most like that thing he had seen in nursery school.

We must respect the fact that what we call the creative cannot be simplistically 'included' in a rationalistically based 'program.' Art schools do not of necessity make painters, although a significant number of them may, variously, come to be there. But that is not *why* they are painters—if they are. We must respect equally the fact that we do *not* know why people are painters, or composers, or poets. In usual, mundane reality, to be any of those 'things' is not a simple, nor even desirable, situation of experience. My mother, with very gentle discretion, used to say, "I like to think that Bob *could* get a job if he had to." Olson's advice, "Poets, you should get a job . . ." makes clear the other side of this vacancy, if by 'poet' one proposes some idealistic creature who is too tender to manage the harsh buffetings of 'real life.' There must be *some* place to live in, together, and if poets tend to get people overexcited, emotionally, as Plato felt, then we simply have to take that chance. We must know by this time that reason, often, can only excuse itself, and it really doesn't seem to be an *initial*—by which I mean a 'first time'—situation in experience. Gregory Corso used to say to people who invited him up to their penthouses for a closer look, "Why don't you just give me the money and let me go home." The creative is frequently a situation of that order, but it isn't a question of, "Give me the tools and I will do the job." Poets have got the tools. They just want to live a little.

So there is this world one thinks of, and another, no doubt, that seems to be there no matter. Jung called them the *creatura,* significantly enough, and the *pleroma,* the first being the mind's world, the world of ideas, differences, distinctions, thought, and the second, the world of physical event purely, having no 'idea' of itself, no 'imagination,' no this or that. Having *two* things, worlds or whatever, the mind wants to ask immediately, which one is *better*—or rather, the *Western* mind does. But you have to give up that 'better,' it just doesn't work—or of course you can go on being a sternly humanistic rationalist, but it won't get you *here.* Because *there* will always be here too, to really drive you out of your head.

One wants to keep growing. One looks for whatever signs seem the issue of that possibility. The plans are to secure that situation, but the hope may be a sad one. I don't want to say that there's no use in living in whatever imagination of the universe is your own. Democracy is literal and will tell you where you are inexorably. You know the people and they know you. Each day, night, you are alive will be specific, even if you are in some body state that seems altogether inaccessible to the others. 'Creative,' as actuality, is here always, never elsewhere in any sense.

I think that where my own confusion lies, in trying to think of 'creative' as an adjective, as some *descriptive* term, is in the fact that I cannot conceive of 'creative' as something available to an attitude of discreet choice—as though

one were able to agree or not, as its interest quickened or
waned in one's thought of it. Life continues as it makes
more life? Is that the self-growth principle? Are we a circumstance of cells having as limit the ability to exhaust the
environment in which we find ourselves? "Well met by
moonlight . . ." A dream of universe that has affections,
qualities, and kinds. How did we get here, like they say.
I was born some years ago and I have paid attention as I
was able, to all that came to attention. I'm an honest man,
I pay what I owe. He was speaking in some heat, irritated
that those who listened to him were not apparently impressed. "How can we tell the dancer from the dance . . ."
Who was it that wanted to. Olson's sense, that art is the
only true twin life has—it 'means nothing,' it doesn't have a
point. The painter Arakawa's delight in *zero set*, the real
nitty gritty for any head-trip. Or—wanted to forget it, get
out of the whole demand. On automatic pilot. Is that
'the creative.'

Basil Bunting said his own recognition, that he was to
be a poet, *was*, in fact, came to him while sitting on the
hearth at the age of four or so, listening to his parents talk
about the Russian-Japanese conflict. It was only hard, he
said, because he didn't know clearly what a *poet* was. Does
one only say that later. I don't think so. I don't think it's
really any different than the recognition that D.D.T. has
such harsh effect on the environment—an *idea* become sub-
stantial, something's really having happened. Richard Alpert
told of a man's jumping off a four story building, then
dying, smiling through blood, in the street. He said the man
must have been happy—*smiling*. Is it discreet, this life. It is
discrete. The *growth* must have multiple phase, like water
boiling or freezing, must have multiple condition, transfer—
transformed to other energy, agency. Eat it up—is eaten.
The farmer feeds the horse a little less each day until he
arrives at that point where the horse is subsisting on nothing
at all. Succeeds, then—but the horse dies. There is no *reason*
why the idea should not be successful, with or without the

horse. It only depends on what you want.

Seeds dormant thousands of years, given chance, luck, might—could—did grow. They eat the flesh of the mammoth frozen millennia, in ice. Hold it! They got the picture. Article in old *Reader's Digest:* "New Hope for the Dead." Simple-minded con trip deigns to speak of 'the rest of us.'

If I could just create the kind of world I'd really like to live in . . . *I* wouldn't be there. 'I' is an experience of creation, which puts up with it no matter. There's a lot to get done. You've been born and that's the first and last ticket. Already he changes his mind, makes the necessary adjustments, picks up his suitcase and getting into his car, drives slowly home. He lives with people whom he has the experience of loving. It all works out. He says. It has to. One to a customer. It's late. But they'll be there. He relaxes. He has an active mind.

•

FOR MY MOTHER: GENEVIEVE JULES CREELEY

April 9, 1887—October 7, 1972

> Tender, semi-
> articulate flickers
> of your
>
> presence, all
> those years
> past
>
> now, eighty-
> five, impossible to
> count them
>
> one by one, like
> addition, sub-
> traction, missing
>
> not one. The last

curled up, in
on yourself,

position you take
in the bed, hair
wisped up

on your head, a
top knot, body
skeletal, eyes

closed against,
it must be,
further disturbance—

breathing a skim
of time, lightly
kicks the intervals—

days, days and
years of it,
work, changes,

sweet flesh caught
at the edges,
dignity's faded

dilemma. It
is *your* life, oh
no one's

forgotten anything
ever. They want
to make you

happy when
they remember. Walk
a little, get

up, now, die
safely,

easily, into

singleness, too
tired with it
to keep

on and one.
Waves break at
the darkness

under the road, sounds
in the faint
night's softness. Look

at them, catching
the light, white
edge as they turn—

always again
and again. Dead
one, two,

three hours—
all these minutes
pass. Is it,

was it, ever
you alone
again, how

long you kept
at it, your
pride, your

lovely, confusing
discretion. Mother, I
love you—for

whatever that
means,
meant—more

than I know, body
gave me my
own, generous,

inexorable place
of you. I feel
the mouth's sluggish-

ness, slips on
turns of things
said, to you,

too soon, too late,
wants to
go back to beginning,

smells of the hospital
room, the doctor
she responds

to now, the
order—get me
there. "Death's

let you out—"
comes true,
this, that,

endlessly circular
life, and we
came back

to see you one
last
time, this

time? Your head
shuddered,
it seemed, your

eyes wanted,

I thought,
to see

who it was.
I am here,
and will follow.

Bolinas, California
October 15, 1972

Inside Out

Notes on the Autobiographical Mode
—for Jane Brakhage

> I'm telling you a
> story to let myself
> think about it. All
>
> day I've been
> here, and yesterday.
> The months, years,
>
> enclose me as
> this thing with arms
> and legs. And if
>
> it *is* time
> to talk about it
> who knows better
>
> than I?

There was a time—primary but not primitive—when experience of consciousness did not separate it from the sensory and perceptive as an agency somehow isolated from those other situations of experience. I mean, the concept and location of *mind* is relatively 'new' to us as people. Some obviously felt it a significant step forward, as Bruno Snell in his book *The Discovery of the Mind.* Others were less happy, feeling that the isolation, thus, of the mind in body, and its use as a *decision*, call it, for all that otherwise constitutes body information, overweighted the *mental* as against what I'll call the *physical.*

Mental and *physical* are aspects, clearly, of one primary unit or organism called a human. But, curious now to realize, there was a time when the eye saw, the hand held, the skin felt, ear heard, nose smelled, etc., each in a primary input to the body as total organism. There was no debate, so to speak—the thought occurred in the experience: Bang! Once mind could think of itself, and so propose an extensive condition of its own function, these primary inputs— and they must remain so, no matter what's 'thought'—seemingly yielded to the mind's activity. Thus, if one were cold, the trick was 'not to think of it' or else 'to think one was not *very* cold,' hence warmer than one was apparently feeling.

I love these tricks of the mind, yet feel increasingly uneasy concerning the impact upon us of their authority. A few years ago Tuli Kupferberg promoted a lovely, if terrifying, slogan: Kill For Peace. How could that be? Well, you had these bad guys, that is, one *thought* they were 'bad,' and these good guys, similarly created, and if you killed all the bad guys, then of course the good guys were 'free'— as they had been to kill—to live in peace. Get the appropriate context and anything in the world can be very simply thought of as 'true.' I smoke, for example, not because it may give me cancer and kill me, but because I like to, or I have it as a habit, or I think it gives my hands and mouth something to do. I—what I experience as *my mind* thinking of *me*—have no problem in removing the causes of possible distress. After all, it's only my body that dies in any case. My mind never will, etc.

Auto-bio-graphy I translate as a life tracking itself. One interesting factor here is that *bios* (life) did not initially extend to *animal* life but was involved with human only. Later, in compounds, its meaning is made to cover organic life in general: biology. It would seem that even at this point life had something very significantly to do with life thinking of itself. What is my life to me? Is it a good life? Organic or animal life *happened*. It could be acted upon, even obliterated—like the dodo bird, but its occasion seemed inextricably involved with its event. There's a large lion in the forest, said the man to his wife whom he had thought of one night in April and thus married. It's me, she said, looking at him. What does it mean: there's a large lion, anywhere, and has anybody told the lion?

I want to think for a while, of anything. Say birds—I like them. People—terrific, if they like me. What a great life we're having, if comfortable in our seats and minds and hearts. Or horrible,—rejected, unloved, in pain. I want to think it over. And over and over and over. Will thinking get me anywhere? To Detroit, possibly. Or here, for those of us who came from elsewhere, truly another abstraction.

In fact, it was that we could haul *it* away, like some ultimate garbage crew, that we came to be here at all, in this place with heads alert to learn, aching for information: The New-s. Abstraction, that yanking from one thing—call it organic life—just enough of it to let it still be there some-how, like the Venus de Milo, and then to use the arms to indicate the whole, so to speak. Obviously she was a lovely woman and her arms were really great to have around you. Once home, with them safely tucked into bed beside you, it possibly occurred to us, as to you, that something precisely to be desired had been left behind.

So what happened? That's where one possibility of the autobiographical can clearly enter. Try to remember. Statue. Arms. You. What did you do with them? What day was it, or night? Think. We'll give you all the time you need. "Lives of great men all remind us/ we can make our lives sublime/ and departing leave behind us/ footsteps (prints?) on (in?) the sands of time . . ." I can't remember. Simply write as clearly as you can what you think was the situation. It's *your* life.

Or, paradoxically, it may have little at all to do with memory. Or let's say, memory is a source of material, fantasy as well as fact. I remember! "I remember, I remember/ the house where I was born . . ." Like a movie my wife told me of in the old days, of doctor coming home in carriage with horse through driving rain, finally pushing his way through **door** into house, wife all excited and waiting for his first words, which are: Tonight history was made. I have just delivered Louis Pasteur!

You begin at any point, and move from that point forward or backward, up or down—or in a direction you yourself choose. In and out of the system, as Buckminster Fuller would say. It's a system—of valuation, habit, complex organic data, the weather, and so on. Usually the choice is to track it backward, that is, most autobiographical impulse tends to follow this course. One can think of **one**'s life as not worth remembering, in fact one can want to forget it— but if what has constituted it, the things "of which it was made up," as William Carlos Williams says, are dear to your memory and experience of them, then it may well be a record of them, a graph of their activity as 'your life,' is an act you would like to perform.

This mode of autobiography is close to our usual senses of history, *his story* as we said in the fourth grade, and it is also useful here to note *history* comes from a Greek root, *'istorin*: to go find out for yourself. This was Charles Olson's clear point of emphasis in his own procedures, that *self-action*—the middle voice—**was** crucial in human existence. Why he so insisted, I think, comes of his belief that humans get truly lost in thought and language insofar as no substantiating act, particularly from and of and to the human itself, takes place. You can't be taught if you won't learn—just like the horse who won't for whatever reason drink.

So here then is possibly a motive, as well as a mode,

for a kind of autobiography that might well be interesting
to any of us. Olson also said, we do what we know before
we know what we do. That's deeply interesting to me—it's
where our bodies return to our minds, among other things.
I feel a threat, not a pleasure, in Descartes' statement: I
think, therefore I am—if that experience is felt to be somehow the most significiant thing we can do. Again it's the
situation of the abstract that I am uneasy about, that
we can be here as *thought*, and that we will so *be*, with primary reality—which of course we also have thought—no
matter what else may prove our actual state of being. Or it
may be that he was just defining the word 'I'—that *I* thinks,
and *me* is otherwise the case.

Me leaves many traces. Diter Rot made works of art
the accumulation of what *me*-ness in the physical world is:
rooms or apartments which slowly filled with casual input,
bags, papers, garbage, junk, and when they were no longer
habitable, being simply too full, he sealed them, then left,
deeming them actual in a way another record of his existence within them could not accomplish. Another man suggested taking daily pictures of one's physical self, face or
whatever, at a photomat, say, so that a 'track' of that aspect of one's life might be documented for referral. In each
case it would seem that the point is not the *thought* of
one's life but rather the *fact* which no situation of 'I' can
gainsay.

Autobiography in this circumstance might be very interesting indeed. You know the way people say, we all have
a story within us—something specific in our lives that would,
could we only get it said, be something worth hearing.
That may well be true but I don't think art is particularly
involved by it. Writing, for example, is an activity dependent on words as material. It may be *felt* that it matters
what they 'say' but far more decisive is the energy gained
in the field or system they are used to create. *Small ham-
bones* versus *big beef cutlets*. That is, you may *see* literal
things thus suggested, but you are hearing also a system of

sounds and rhythms that these materials are effectually creating. In like sense, the "Chef's Special" may sound good to you—but it may be awful to literally eat, and you won't know what it is until someone who does know tells you.

Again—stop it all. The boat's left, it's gone, nothing comes back from that place. You can run the film backward but it won't be the same. E.g., Ken Mikolowski has a lovely poem simply of the fact you can reverse linear patterns: *Oh say can you see* becoming *See you can say oh.* Time is either an imagination or else a phasing inherent in the system, organic or inert (including abstractions). What *is* your life that you're going to write it down, or make films of it, or whatever it is you had in mind. The one thing clear about your life is that you are living it. You're here—wherever that is. Whitman was quick about it, saying, "Who touches this book touches a man." He knew that whoever was holding the book to read it would physically be there. And that, believe it or not, is really fast thinking. I write *these words*, muttering, thinking, to myself. Cross fingers *and* I may well be dead before I ever chance to read them to you—a powerful and dangerous thing ever to say even to oneself. Witness what the words have done to *me* as *I* gains locus.

We—that unimaginable *plural* of I!—want our lives to be known to us, we don't want it all a seeming dream, back to Plato's cave again. We want the *light*—even a rock band or particularly a rock band *called* Plato's Cave, if nothing else seems to get it on. We don't want to hang around waiting to be x'ed out at some 'later date.' Henry M. Yaker writes: "Certain primitive cultures have no past or future tense in their language, and express all events of life, real or mythological, in an 'eternal now' . . ." That sounds fair enough. Everybody's here at this point, and they always were—despite the lack of communication. Of course a 'we' will still be found to flood thousands of acres of forest at the headwater of the Amazon, regretting they haven't means to inform the divers people living in those forests of the impending 'event.' That's another mode of autobiography, 'think big.' This will really get them in Des Moines. And so I tell you, friends and neighbors, although I come from humble origins, early in life I took the big chances— and won. You want to work for someone like that? Don't— even if you have to. Fuck him up, like they say. He's taken everything else.

Is autobiography, at least the written, just a means of self-justification, the 'facts' that excuse you? A few days ago in New York I got five parking tickets in forty-eight hours. When I put that into my linear patterning, it fair broke my mind—and I felt like leaving for California that very night. The car, happily, was already there, viz. California license plates—so, *I'll* be back. But not always to say, gee, I'm sorry, or, wasn't it nice yesterday. Shucks.

Too often we are told to generalize ourselves in the pattern of an idea that may or may not have specific relevance for what we feel as persons otherwise. The *imagination* of a commonwealth must make that sharing literal— there cannot be an invested partiality hidden from the participants. When the New York Police Department has persons within it who will literally threaten to run other persons down with trucks in order to gain their compliance, no matter how 'guilty' those threatened may be, one cannot accept the agency. Realize that the *general*, the *we-ness* proposed in various realities, may well prove to be this kind. Obviously any 'we' must, willynilly, submit to the organic orders of its existence: must sleep, must eat, must drink, must move, must die. But that is very nearly the totality of the actual demand. Elsewise, the 'geography leans in,' as Olson put it. Place is a real event—where you are is a law equal to what you are.

To discover a precison in this situation, to act in the specific context, takes all the wit and alertness any one of us can bring to it. You'll recognize that people tend to check one another out, coming from divers places. With hitchhikers a few nights ago, I had an extraordinary infor-

mation of routes that can move us across this country, by-
passes, numbers, weather, places—and the people to be met
with in every major nexus of persons from here to L.A.
Time as well was particular—as it is insistently for the
Guatemalan Indians, who have a precise vocabulary of explicit measures for the way in which you are moving—on
foot, say, or on horseback, truck, etc. And these are *not*
interchangeable, only translatable.

What the autobiographic does, primarily, is to specify
person—at least it has that capability. Reading, for example,
Mandelstam's widow's book, *Hope Against Hope,* persons
become actual—there is no generality of impression such
as, Russia is hostile to the Jews. A literal man is demonstrated as experiencing a viciously insistent persecution, finally resulting in his death. One can, of course, feel the report exaggerated, simply that it is his widow who relates
the story. But *her* words are again, literally, a *person* saying
them. You, as person also, can make up your own mind—
and the question isn't one inviting you to feel that poetry
in Russia should be more respected. The fact is, it *is* respected—so much so that Mandelstam dies *because* the power of his gift is so feared. Think: scrawled on the wall of a
death camp by someone waiting to die, a *line* of Mandelstam's, one not even to be found in a so-called book but
carried in the ear, mind and mouth, person to person, all
that bitter distance.

One time, years ago now, Allen Ginsberg was at a party in New York talking with a young woman about the apparent hostility publishers then felt toward the younger
American poets, myself in particular. She was, as it happens,
a junior editor at Harper's, and listened patiently to his irritation. Then she said, we've been in business for over
eighty years and I think we know what we're doing. At
which point Ginsberg naturally flipped—You? *You've* been
in business for over eighty years? Why you're only twenty-
two years old!

Why not speak for yourself. Sooner or later you'll have

to. There are no sure investments. Watch the dollar do the dirty float—like a mind, a dead idea, fading out.

I'm tired and I want to stop this mumbling. But I've made a commitment, and I want to respect it. That's true. What other experience of 'I' is interesting, except that which manifests its patterning, the laws of its own imagination and possible experience. Tell me who I am. Amnesia, but the person continues eating, sleeping, begins again. In group therapy investments of the experience of 'I' are relinquished, even forced out. Richard Alpert recalled his first experience of LSD as being a loss of all ego support—his sense of himself as a brilliant young psychologist, a professor at Harvard, a successful son, and much more, melted like ice in hot sun. Can you melt yourself, 'autobiographically,' can you stand, literally, not to be some absent dream of glory, just what your mother always wanted.

Or consider Gregory Corso's reaction to people talking about the joys of ego loss: lose your egos? You're not even good enough to *have* egos. Agh.

So keep on tracking—life. "To measure is all we know . . ." You want to use somebody else's ruler, that's your business. I don't know that all the emphasis upon individual sensibility isn't some simple con game, simply 'divide and conquer.' But who *are* you, and why does your life propose itself as a collective. Is it a premise got from the fact we constitute a species, 'we are many'—which is certainly attractive to any *me* of myself I can experience as *I*. There's no pleasure in being by yourself finally, always alone.

I love the possibly apocryphal account of nineteenth century people in Russia going up to absolute strangers in the street, grabbing them by the knees, and then confessing to them some incredible act. Like Dostoyevsky's account of the rape of a child with which he had been involved. Or Ginsberg saying to the old poet in Peru, I want to know your dirtiest secrets. We've had a lot to do with those 'secrets,' lately. In the My Lai inquiry soldiers told humanly awful stories in seemingly unquestioning tones of voice—such as giving a pesty kid a spam sandwich with a thermal device inside it, which then flared in the kid's throat and stomach, killing him. What gave them containment was the *general* —the United States Army in this instance. You give each of the six men of the firing squad a gun, only one of which has a live bullet. You shuffle the guns first of all, so that even you can't identify the lethal weapon. Then you check your own commands, and then you give the order to shoot. No one has killed anyone, specifically—he's just dropped dead. Suddenly I think of the *general* of an army, old Mr. Abstraction himself. Ours not to reason why—ours just to do it, and let those mothers die.

Autobiography might be thought of, then, as some sense of a life *responsive* to its own experience of itself. This is the 'inside out,' so to speak—somehow reminiscent of, It ain't no sin/ to take off your skin/ and dance around in your boh-hones . . . Trying to take a look, see what it was all about, why Mary never came home and Joe was, after all, your best friend. Not to explain—that is, not to lay a trip on them—rather an *evidence* seems what one is trying to get hold of, to have use of oneself specifically as something that *does* something, and in so doing leaves a record, a consequence, intentionally or not.

The sculptor Marisol speaks of using herself, over and over, in her work. "When I show myself as I am I return to reality." When one wears a uniform or otherwise generalizes the condition of one's experience of oneself, that "reality" is most difficult to enter. There was, sadly, a professor employed at the University of New Mexico who one time began a lecture with the statement: As I was shaving this morning, seeing myself in the mirror, Professor Jones, I said . . . That is the end of the story, just another professor, no one otherwise home. There can be a different experience of that situation as one of the earliest discovered occasions of written language makes clear: I, John, foreman of Pit 7, hereby testify . . . Or words to that effect. This is the responsibility of identity, not its specious investment.

57

Do you *know* how to drive the car, *can* you stop this bleeding, *are* you a competent doctor, lawyer, teacher, father—or are you just out to lunch.

Thère must be times when the experience of being oneself is almost unendurable—by which I mean, something has happened, oneself being the agency, and it is unspeakably difficult to accept *what* one has thus done. Williams, a markedly autobiographical writer, spoke of poems as "capsules wherein we wrap up our punishable secrets." That is a Puritan sense certainly, but Puritans have been great practitioners of autobiography—Thoreau, D.H. Lawrence and Edward Dahlberg among them. Any context which makes one feel singular in life, a specific isolated consciousness in the universe, intensifies the attraction of this situation of statement. Camus' first draft of *The Stranger* uses an *I* which is markedly himself, I am told, and certainly 'existentialism' is a Puritan stance.

No doubt there are clear signs of a kind of paranoia in this mode, just that the *I* feels itself surrounded by a *they* to which its experience of itself cannot easily refer. Paranoia in the arts is by no means unfamiliar. The artist must often feel that he or she has been deliberately cut off from some generality of social grouping, and so must both state, and implicitly justify, the fact of his or her 'life'. Since no one else apparently cares, I will speak of myself to myself. I know that I, as an artist, have never dared to imagine in working that an actual audience might be literally attentive to what I have to say. Therefore my primary experience of an audience has been my own eye, or ear, listening to what it was that was being said. My wife tells me that I often mutter when writing, and also frequently laugh—both instances of the situation I am describing. Now, older, when I am at times asked to say something specifically to an audience, I am still dependent primarily on what I hear in saying it, not what the audience may hear. In that respect I am very thick-skinned, and can take a good deal of abuse, as long as that which is getting said is of interest to me. Another situation of statement would obviously stop, confounded, when it found that response, apart from its own experience of itself, was hostile.

When Angus Fletcher speaks of the change in the *imagination* of how persons may experience the world, from Marlowe to Bunyan, say, he is emphasizing the shift in consciousness from a communal locus to a singular one, to an *I* that has discovered the possibility of its own assumption of the *right*, self-defined and self-asserted, to be an *I* co-present and equal in that sense to all other possibilities of reality. It is a giddy moment, and perhaps a deeply tragic one. Bunyan, despite the fact that *Pilgrim's Progress* uses the *form* of autobiography, is far indeed from its literal experience as we would now define it. He is a deeply communal man and cannot speak as *one*. Marlowe, on the other hand, seems very present in *Dr. Faustus*—we think of *his* literal life, witnessing that play. With Goethe, we are in a different 'place' entirely, far closer to social 'mythology.'

It is Castaneda who 'autobiographically' tells us of Don Juan's teachings. Don Juan is not interested in 'himself' in that way, as those teachings, even so filtered, make clear. I think it wise to be aware of this problem, so to speak, insofar as any autobiographical mode can seem to be significant *in itself*—just as the *I* of its creation has assumed, *ipso facto*, that what he or she has to say is significant. If, by *significant*, one means that the statement signifies something, no matter what, then all seems well and good. Anything that happens 'signifies.' But if there is otherwise an intention, an ulterior motive as it's called, then the problem is very much more complex. Is that great man's life, which reminds us, *in itself* directed to do so? That is, did he literally live it for that purpose? Possibly yes. But what he *thought* he was doing, no matter how directed, can never to my mind be as actual or as significant as what he *was*, literally, doing. Which is to say nothing more than that Hitler must have been no less possessed by an *idea* than was Jesus, *and* we know that what affects us is the *event* of that fact in each case.

When people are very old, and there is the consciousness of death coming upon them, a very marked impulse to
tell what their lives have been occurs. I don't think it is simply loneliness in that situation, or that they have lost otherwise a *place*. The grandfathers, and grandmothers, are the
great storytellers—and in societies alert to that human need
they are of course so used. They tell a life of *I* that becomes more than singular consciousness in isolations of intent or assertive energy. They are, as it were, taking the *I*
back to its center. Olson once told me that the initial sign
for the pronoun *I* was a boat. Insofar as *I* is a vehicle of
passage or transformation, its powers are clear. Realized as
will or personality, that 'mealy seal' as Olson called it, the
power vitiates as soon as the energy necessary to sustain it
exhausts itself. 'L'état, c'est moi' is truly the end of a period.

Those of us who came of age in the forties remember
the extraordinary turmoil within human consciousness,
which was, on the one hand, the Second World War, and,
on the other, existentialism. We saw what Jung might call
the 'individuation process' enter the nightmare of 'divided
creation,' torn from centers of physical reality. The heroism
of Allen Ginsberg in the fifties cannot be overemphasized:
"*I* saw the best minds of my generation destroyed by mad-
ness, starving, hysterical . . ." Come *back* into the body. We
do not go 'backward' or 'forward' in the mind—we live and
die. Olson, dying, was relieved, almost to delight, that the
fundament, that physical *thing* we are, had not been lost in
the *firmament,* that *mind* world of stars and extensions.

What can one do? "Tell the story." "To tell/ what subsequently I saw and what heard/ —to place myself (in/ my
nature) beside nature/ to imitate nature (for to copy nature
would be a/ shameful thing)/ I lay myself down . . ."

To bear witness. To be here, to hear. To tell.

Buffalo, N.Y.
March 22, 1973

Introduction to
Penguin *Selected Whitman*

One of the most lovely insistences in Whitman's poems seems to me his instruction that one speak for oneself. Assumedly that would be the person most involved in saying anything and yet a habit of 'objective' statement argues the contrary, noting the biases and distortions and tediums of the personal that are thereby invited into the writing. Surely there is some measure possible, such would say, that can make statement a clearly defined and impersonal instance of reality, of white clouds in a blue sky, or things and feelings not distorted by any fact of one man or woman's intensive possession of them. Then there would truly be a common possibility, that all might share, and that no one would have use of more than another.

Yet if Whitman has taught me anything, and he has taught me a great deal, often against my own will, it is that the common *is* personal, intensely so, in that having no one thus to invest it, the sea becomes a curious mixture of water and table salt and the sky the chemical formula for air. It is, paradoxically, the personal which makes the common insofar as it recognizes the existence of the many in the one. In my own joy or despair, I am brought to that which others have also experienced.

My own senses of Whitman were curiously numb until I was thirty. In the forties, when I was in college, it was considered literally bad taste to have an active interest in his writing. In that sense he suffered the same fate as Wordsworth, also condemned as overly prolix and generalizing. There was a persistent embarrassment that this naively affirmative poet might affect one's own somewhat cynical wisdoms. Too, insofar as this was a time of intensively didactic criticism, what was one to do with Whitman, even if one read him? He went on and on, he seemed to lack 'structure,' he yielded to no 'critical apparatus' then to hand. So, as students, we were herded past him as quickly as possible, and our teachers used him only as an example of 'the America of that period' which, we were told, was a vast swamp of idealistic expansion and corruption. Whitman, the dupe, the dumbbell, the pathetically regrettable instance of this country's dream and despair, the self-taught man.

That summation of Whitman and his work was a very comfortable one for all concerned. If I felt at times awkward with it, I had only to turn to Ezra Pound, whom the university also condemned, to find that he too disapproved despite the begrudging 'Pact.' At least he spoke of having 'detested' Whitman, only publicly altering the implications of that opinion in a series of BBC interviews made in the late fifties. William Carlos Williams also seemed to dislike him, decrying the looseness of the writing, as he felt it, and the lack of a coherent prosody. He as well seemed to change his mind in age insofar as he referred to Whitman as the greatest of American poets in a public lecture on American poetry for college students. Eliot also changes his mind, as did James before him, but the point is that the heroes of my youth as well as my teachers were almost without exception extremely critical of Whitman and his influence and wanted as little as possible to do with him.

Two men, however, most dear to me, felt otherwise. The first of these was D.H. Lawrence, whose *Studies in*

Classic American Literature remains the most extraordinary apprehension of the nature of American experience and writing that I know. His piece on Whitman in that book is fundamental in that he, in a decisively personal manner, first castigates Whitman for what he considers a muddling assumption of 'oneness,' citing "I am he that aches with amorous love . . ." as particularly offensive, and then, with equal intensity, applauds that Whitman who is, as he puts it, "a great charger of the blood in men," a truly heroic poet whose vision and will make a place of absolute communion for others.

The second, Hart Crane, shared with Whitman my own teachers' disapproval. I remember a course which I took with F. O. Matthiessen, surely a man of deep commitment and care for his students, from which Crane had been absented. I asked for permission to give a paper on Crane, which he gave me, but I had overlooked what I should have realized would be the response of the class itself, understandably intent upon its own sophistications. How would they accept these lines, for example?

> yes, Walt,
> Afoot again, and onward without halt,—
> Not soon, nor suddenly,—no, never to let go
> My hand
> in yours,
> Walt Whitman—
> so—

If they did not laugh outright at what must have seemed to them the awkwardly stressed rhymes and sentimental camaraderie, then they tittered at Crane's will to be one with his fellow *homosexual*. But didn't they hear, I wanted to insist, the pacing of the rhythms of those lines, the syntax, the intently human tone, or simply the punctuation? Couldn't they read? Was Crane to be simply another 'crudity' they could so glibly be rid of? But still I myself didn't read Whitman, more than the few poems of his that were 'dealt with' in classes or that some friend asked me to. No doubt I too was embarrassed by my aunt's and my grandmother's ability to recite that terrible poem, "O Captain! My Captain!," banal as I felt it to be, and yet what was that specious taste which could so distract any attention and could righteously dismiss so much possibility, just because it didn't 'like' it? Sadly, it was too much my own.

So I didn't really read Whitman for some years although from time to time I realized that the disposition toward his work must be changing. Increasing numbers of articles began to appear as, for one example, Randall Jarrell's "Whitman Revisited." But the import of this writing had primarily to do with Whitman's work as instance of social history or else with its philosophical basis or, in short, with all that did not attempt to respect the technical aspects of his writing, his prosody and the characteristic method of his organization within the specific poems.

It was, finally, the respect accorded Whitman by three of my fellow poets that began to impress me as not only significant to their various concepts of poetry but as unmistakable evidence of his basic use to any estimation of the nature of poetry itself. I had grown up, so to speak, habituated to the use of poetry as compact, epiphanal instance of emotion or insight. I valued its intensive compression, its ability to 'get through' a maze of conflict and confusion to some center of clear 'point.' But what did one do if the emotion or terms of thought could not be so focused upon or isolated in such singularity? Assuming a context in which the statement was of necessity multiphasic, a circumstance the components of which were multiple, or, literally, a day in which various things *did* occur, not simply one thing—what did one do with that? Allen Ginsberg was quick to see that Whitman's line was of very specific use. As he says in "Notes Written on Finally Recording Howl," "No attempt's been made to use it in the light of early XX Century organization of new speech-rhythm prosody to *build up* large organic structures." The structure of "Howl" itself and of subsequent poems such as "Kaddish" demonstrates to my own mind how much technically Ginsberg had learned from Whitman's method of taking the poem as a 'field,' in Charles Olson's sense, rather than as a discreet line through alternatives to some adamant point of conclusion.

In the work of Robert Duncan the *imagination* of the poem is very coincident with Whitman's. For example, in a contribution to *Poets on Poetry* (1966) Duncan writes:

> We begin to imagine a cosmos in which the poet and the poem are on in a moving process, not only here the given Creation and the Exodus or Fall, but also here the immanence of the Creator in Creation. The most real is given and we have fallen away, but the most real is in the falling revealing itself in what is happening. Between the god *in* the story and the god *of* the story, the form, the realization of what is happening, stirs the poet. To answer that call, to become the poet, means to be aware of creation, creature and creator coinherent in the one event . . .

If one reads the 1855 'Preface' to *Leaves of Grass* in the context here defined, the seeming largenesses of act which Whitman grants to the poet find actual place in that "immanence of the Creator in Creation" which Duncan notes. More, the singular presence of Whitman in Duncan's "A Poem Beginning with a Line by Pindar" is an extraordinary realization of the *measure* Whitman has given us:

> There is no continuity then. Only a few
>   posts of the good remain. I too
> that am a nation sustain the damage
>   where smokes of continual ravage
> obscure the flame.
>   It is across great scars of wrong

I reach toward the song of kindred men
and strike again the naked string
old Whitman sang from. Glorious mistake!
  that cried:

"The theme is creative and has vista."
"He is the president of regulation."

I see always the under side turning,
fumes that injure the tender landscape.
From which up break
lilac blossoms of courage in daily act
  striving to meet a natural measure.

Louis Zukofsky, the third friend thus to instruct me, recalls and transforms Whitman's *Leaves* again and again, as here:

The music is in the flower,
Leaf around leaf ranged around the center;
Profuse but clear outer leaf breaking on space,
There is space to step to the central heart:
The music is in the flower,
It is not the sea but hyaline cushions the flower—
Liveforever, everlasting.
The leaves never topple from each other,
Each leaf a buttress flung for the other.

(from '*A*' 2, 1928)

I have no way of knowing if those lines directly refer to Whitman's *Leaves of Grass* and yet, intuitively, I have no doubt of it whatsoever. Zukofsky once told me that, for him, the eleventh section of "Song of Myself" constituted the American *Shih King*, which is to say, it taught the possibilities of what might be said or sung in poetry with that grace of technical agency, or mode, thereby to accomplish those possibilities. *It presents*. It does not talk about or refer to—in the subtlety of its realization, it becomes real.

It is also Zukofsky who made me aware of Whitman's power in an emotion I had not associated with him—a deeply passionate anger. Zukofsky includes an essay called "Poetry" in the first edition of "*A*" *1-12,* at the end of which he quotes the entire text of "Respondez!," a poem which Whitman finally took out of *Leaves of Grass* in 1881 but which I have put in this selection, as singular instance of that power and in respect to the man who made me aware of it.

Then, in the late fifties, I found myself embarrassed for proper academic credentials although I was teaching at the time, and so went back to graduate school, to get the appropriate degree. One of the first courses I took in that situation was called "Twain and Whitman," taught by John Gerber, who was a visiting professor at the University of New Mexico from Iowa State. One thing he did with us I remember very well—he asked us to do a so-called thematic outline of "Song of Myself." The room in which we met had large blackboards on all four walls and on the day they were due, we were told to copy our various outlines on to the blackboards. So we all got up and did so. When we finally got back to our seats, we noticed one very striking fact. No two of the outlines were the same—which was Professor Gerber's very instructive point. Whitman did not write with a systematized logic of 'subject' nor did he 'organize' his materials with a logically set schedule for their occurrence in the poem. Again the situation of a 'field' of activity, rather than some didactic imposition of a 'line' of order, was very clear.

At that same time I became interested in the nature of Whitman's prosody and looked through as many scholarly articles concerning it as I could find in the university library. None were really of much use to me, simply that the usual academic measure of such activity depends upon the rigid presumption of a standardized metrical system, which is, at best, the hindsight gained from a practice far more fluid in its own occasion. Sculley Bradley (co-editor with Harold W.

Blodgett of the best text for Whitman's poems available to my knowledge: *Leaves of Grass,* Comprehensive Reader's Edition, New York University Press, 1965) did speak of a *variable stress* or *foot,* that is, a hovering accent, or accents, within clusters of words in the line, that did not fall in a statically determined pattern but rather shifted with the impulse of the statement itself. This sense of the stress pattern in Whitman's poems was interestingly parallel to William Carlos Williams' use of what he also called "the variable foot" in his later poems, so that the periodicity of the line, its duration in time, so to speak, stayed in the general pattern constant but the stress or stresses within the unit of the line itself were free to move with the condition of the literal things being said, both as units of semantic information, e.g., "I am the chanter . . . ," or as units of sound and rhythm, e.g., "I chant copious the islands beyond . . ." It is, of course, impossible ever to separate these two terms in their actual function, but it is possible that one will be more or less concerned with each in turn in the activity of writing. More simply, I remember one occasion in high school when I turned a 'unit' primarily involved with sounds and rhythm into a 'unit' particularly involved with semantic statement, to wit: "Inebriate of air am I . . ." altered in my memory to read, "I am an inebriate of air . . ." My teacher told me I had the most unpoetic ear he'd yet encountered.

Remember that what we call 'rhyming' is the recurrence of a sound sufficiently similar to one preceding it to catch in the ear and mind as being the 'same' and that such sounds can be modified in a great diversity of ways. In the sounding of words themselves the extension seems almost endless: *maid, made, may, mad, mate, wait, say,* etc. Given the initial vowel with its accompanying consonants and also its own condition, i.e., whether it is 'long' or 'short,' one can then play upon that sound as long as one's energy *and* the initial word's own ability to stay in the ear as 'residue' can survive. In verse the weaving and play of such sound is far more complex than any observation of the rhymes at the ends of lines can tabulate.

This kind of rhyming is instance of what one can call *parallelism*, and the parallelism which similarity of sounds can effect is only one of the many alternate sources of 'rhyming' which verse has at hand. For example, there is a great deal of syntactic 'rhyming' in Whitman's poetry, insistently parallel syntactic structures which themselves make a strong web of coherence. There is also the possibility of parallelism in the nature of what is being thought and/or felt as emotion, and this too can serve to increase the experience of coherence in the statement the poem is working to accomplish.

The constantly recurring structures in Whitman's writing, the insistently parallel sounds and rhythms, recall the patterns of waves as I now see them daily. How can I point to *this* wave, or *that* one, and announce that it is *the* one? Rather Whitman's method seems to me a process of sometimes seemingly endless gathering, moving in the energy of his own attention and impulse. There are obviously occasions to the contrary to be found in his work but the basic pattern does seem of this order. I am struck by the fact that William Michael Rossetti in the introduction to his *Poems of Walt Whitman* (1868) speaks of the style as being occasionally "agglomerative," a word which can mean "having the state of a confused or jumbled mass" but which, more literally, describes the circumstance of something "made or formed into a rounded mass or ball." A few days ago here, walking along the beach, a friend showed me such a ball, primarily of clay but equally compacted of shells and pebbles which the action of the waves had caused the clay to pick up, all of which would, in time, become stone. That meaning of "agglomerate" I think particularly relevant to the activity of Whitman's composition, and I like too that sense of the spherical, which does not locate itself upon a point nor have the strict condition of the linear but rather is at all 'points' the possibility of all that it is. Whitman's constant habit of revisions and additions would concur, I think, with this notion of his process, in that there is not 'one thing' to be said and, that done, then 'another.' Rather the process permits the material ('myself' in the world) to extend until literal death intercedes. Again, it is interesting to think of Zukofsky's sense that any of us as poets "write one poem all our lives," remembering that Whitman does not think of his work as a series of discreet collections or books but instead adds to the initial work, *Leaves of Grass,* thinking of it as a "single poem."

The implications of such a stance have a very contemporary bearing for American poets—who can no longer assume either their world or themselves in it as discrete occasion. Not only does Whitman anticipate the American affection for the pragmatic, but he equally emphasizes that it is space and process which are unremittingly our condition. If Pound found the manner of his poems objectionable, he nonetheless comes to a form curiously like *Leaves of Grass* in the *Cantos,* in that he uses them as the literal possibility of a life. Much the same situation occurs in Williams' writing with *Paterson,* although it comes at a markedly later time in his own life. Charles Olson's *Maximus Poems* and Louis Zukofsky's *"A"* are also instances of this form which proposes to 'go on' in distinction to one that assumes its own containment as a singular case.

Another objection Rossetti had concerned what he called "absurd or ill-constructed words" in Whitman's writing. One distinct power a poet may be blessed with is that of *naming* and Whitman's appetite in this respect was large and unembarrassed. One should read a posthumously published collection of notes he wrote on his own sense of words called *An American Primer* (City Lights, 1970), wherein he makes clear his commitment to their power of transformation. Whitman's vocabulary moves freely among an extraordinarily wide range of occupational terminologies and kinds of diction found in divers social groupings. Fre-

quently there are juxtapositions of terms appropriate to
markedly different social or occupational habits, slang sided
with words of an alternate derivation:

I chant the chant of dilation or pride,
We have had ducking and deprecating about enough . . .

Whatever the reader's response, such language permits
Whitman to gain an actively useful diversity of context and
tone. The toughness of his verse—what Charles Olson referred to as its *muscularity,* giving as instance "Trickle
Drops"—can sustain the tensions created in its movement
by these seeming disparities in diction. It is, moreover, a
marked characteristic of American poetry since Whitman,
and certainly of the contemporary, to have no single source
for its language in the sense that it does not depend upon
a 'poetic' or literary vocabulary. In contrast, a German
friend once told me that even a novelist as committed to a
commonly shared situation of life as Günter Grass could
not be easily understood by the workmen whose circumstances so moved him. His language was too literary in its
structure and vocabulary, not by fact of his own choice but
because such language was adamantly that in which novels
were to be written in German. An American may choose, as
John Ashbery once did, to write a group of poems whose
words come entirely from the diction of the *Wall Street
Journal,* but it is his own necessity, not that put upon him
by some rigidity of literary taste.

Comparable to this flexibility of diction in Whitman's
writing is the tone or mood in which his poems speak. It is
very open, familiar, at times very casual and yet able to be,
on the instant, intensive, intimate, charged with complexly
diverse emotion. This manner of address invites, as it were,
the person reading to 'come into' the activity and experience of the poems, to share with Whitman in a paradoxically unsentimental manner the actual texture and force of
the emotions involved. When he speaks directly to the

reader, there is an uncanny feeling of his literal presence physically.

I have avoided discussion of Whitman's life simply because I am not competent to add anything to the information of any simple biography, for example, Gay Wilson Allen's *Walt Whitman* (Evergreen Books, London, 1961). I am charmed by some of the details got from that book. Apparently Mrs. Gilchrist, the widow of Blake's biographer, Alexander Gilchrist, was very smitten upon reading Whitman's poems and wrote accordingly:

> Even in this first letter (3 September, 1871) Mrs. Gilchrist made it plain that she was proposing marriage. She hoped, she said, to hear, 'My Mate. The one I so much want. Bride, Wife, indissoluble eternal!' And, 'Dear Walt. It is a sweet & precious thing, this love: it clings so close, so close to the Soul and Body, all so tenderly dear, so beautiful, so sacred . . .'

It is simple enough to make fun of this lady and yet her response, despite Whitman's very careful demurring, is one that his poems are unequivocally capable of producing. It would be sad indeed if books could not be felt as entirely human and possible occasion.

More to the point, Whitman's life is a very discreet one, really. John Addington Symonds so pestered him concerning "the meaning of the 'Calamus' poems," that Whitman finally answered, "Though unmarried, I have six children . . ." But whether or not that was true, or untrue, or whether Whitman was homosexual, bisexual, or heterosexual, has not primarily concerned me. In other words, I have been intent upon the writing and what there took place and that, literally, is what any of us have now as a possibility. We cannot haul him back any more than we can Shakespeare, just to tell us who he was. It would seem that he *had*, with such magnificent articulation one is almost persuaded there can be no end to him just as there is none to the genius of his writing.

Nor have I been able to do more than gloss the multiplicity of uses I find in the work itself. I wish there were time to think of Whitman as instance of what Allen Ginsberg pointd out as a great tradition of American poets, that of the *crank* or true eccentric. Surely his contemporaries often felt him to be. There is a lovely letter which Gerard Manley Hopkins wrote Bridges, in which he says that Whitman is closer to him in technical concerns than any other poet then writing—but also, that he is a veritable madman, so what does that make poor Hopkins? Or I would like to consider a suggestion of Duncan's, that possibly Williams' uneasiness with Whitman's writing had in part to do with the fact that Williams uses *enjambment*, or 'run-over' lines, very frequently whereas Whitman uses it not at all—wherein he is very like Ezra Pound. Or to trace more carefully the nature of Whitman's influence on American poetry—an influence I find as clearly in Frank O'Hara's poems as I do in Crane's or Ginsberg's.

Undertaking any of this, I felt a sudden giddiness—not at all self-humbling. This man is a *great* poet, our first, and it is unlikely indeed that his contribution to what it literally means to be an *American* poet will ever be equalled. But I do not want to end this note with such blatant emphasis. As Duncan says, Whitman is a deeply gentle man and, humanly, of great, great reassurance. If our America now is a petty shambles of disillusion and violence, the dreams of its possibility stay actual in Whitman's words. It is not 'democracy' that, of itself, can realize or even recognize the common need. It is only, and literally, people themselves who have that choice. So then, as Lawrence said: "Ahead of all poets, pioneering into the wilderness of unopened life, Whitman . . ."

Bolinas, California
January 30, 1972

On the Road:
Notes on Artists & Poets
1950-1965

Coming of age in the forties, in the chaos of the Second
World War, one felt the kinds of coherence that might have
been fact of other time and place were no longer possible.
There seemed no logic, so to speak, that could bring together all the violent disparities of that experience. The arts
especially were shaken and the *picture of the world* that
might previously have served them had to be reformed. Of
course, the underlying information of this circumstance had
begun long before the time with which I am. involved. Once
the containment of a Newtonian imagination of the universe
had been forced to yield to one proposing life as continu-
ous, atomistic, and without relief, then discretions possible
in the first situation were not only inappropriate but increasingly grotesque. There was no *place,* finally, from
which to propose an objectively ordered reality, a world
that could be spoken of as *there* in the convenience of ex-
pectation or habit.

The cities, insofar as they are intensively conglomerate
densities of people, no doubt were forced to recognize the
change previous to other kinds of place. The *neighborhood*
had been changing endlessly, ever since the onslaught of the

Industrial Revolution, and *change,* like it or not, had become so familiar a condition that there was even a dependence on the energy thus occurring. Nothing seemingly held firm and so one was either brought to a depressed and ironically stated pessimism concerning human possibilities, or one worked to gain location in the insistent flux, recognizing the nature of its shifting energies as intimate with one's own.

Put another way, this situation increasingly demanded that the arts, *all* of them—since no matter how disparate their preoccupations may sometimes appear, their roots are always fact of a commonly shared intuition or impulse— that these articulations and perceptions of the nature of human event *yield* the assumption of discrete reality, of objects to be hung on walls merely to be looked at, or words rehearsing agreed to patterns of valuation and order, or sounds maintaining rationally derived systems of coherence; that the human event itself be permitted to enter, again, the most significant of its own self-realizations.

Hindsight makes all such statement far more tidy than it ever in fact was or could be. As a young man trying to get a purchase on what most concerned me—the issue of my own life and its statement in writing—I knew little if anything of what might be *happening.* I had gone through a usual education in the east, had witnessed in shock the terrifying conclusion of humans killing one another, had wobbled back to college, married (mistakenly) in the hope of securing myself emotionally, had wandered into the woods just that I had no competence to keep things together in the city, even left the country itself, with my tolerant wife, hoping that some other culture might have news for me I could at last make use of and peace with. But the world, happily or unhappily, offers only one means of leaving, and I was returned without relief again and again to the initial need: a *means* of making articulate the world in which I and all like me did truly live.

Most stable in these preoccupations was the sense that

any *form,* any ordering of reality so implied, had somehow to come from the very condition of the experience demanding it. That is to say, I could not easily use a previous mode of writing that wasn't consequence of my own literal experience. I couldn't write like Eliot, for example, I couldn't even depend upon Stevens, whose work then much attracted me. So it was that I became increasingly drawn to the proposals of Ezra Pound ("We must understand what is happening . . .") and to the work of William Carlos Williams:

> From disorder (a chaos)
> order grows
> —grows fruitful.
> The chaos feeds it. Chaos
> feeds the tree.

> *(Descent)*

Then, in 1950, a chance contact with Charles Olson gained through a mutual friend, Vincent Ferrini, changed my mind entirely and gave me access at last to a way of thinking of the process of writing that made both the thing said and the way of saying it an integral event. More, Olson's relation to Black Mountain College (which led to my own) found me that company I had almost despaired of ever having. So put, my emphasis here seems almost selfishly preoccupied with *me*—but I was, after all, one of many, all of whom had many of these same feelings and dilemmas. I expect that one of the first tests of the artist is his or her ability to maintain attention and activity in an environment having apparently very little concern or interest in what seems so crucial to oneself. *Company,* then, is a particularly dear and productive possibility for anyone so committed. Mine was answer to every wish I had ever had.

Living in Europe, in France and then in Mallorca, I had come to know some painters, like they say. Ezra Pound had generously put me in touch with René Laubiès, the first to translate selections from the *Cantos* into French, and I found him a warm and intelligent friend. However, I felt rather gauche and heavy around his work, which was in some respects an extension of usual School of Paris preoccupations—that is, he did work to realize a thing in mind, a *sign* or *symbol* that had value for him apart from its occasion in the work itself. His dealer was Paul Fachetti, happily, and it was at this gallery I first saw Jackson Pollock's work, a show of small canvasses giving some sense of the *mode* but without the *scale* that finally seems crucial for him. In any case, these paintings stuck in my head very firmly so that even now I can recall them without difficulty. Lawrence Calcagno and Sam Francis were also showing at Fachetti's, but neither made much impression on me at the time, despite I was delighted they were Americans.

Possibly I hadn't as yet realized that a number of American painters had made the shift I was myself so anxious to accomplish, that they had, in fact, already begun to move away from the insistently *pictorial,* whether figurative or non-figurative, to a manifest directly of the *energy* inherent in the materials, literally, and their physical manipulation in the act of painting itself. *Process,* in the sense that Olson had found it in Whitehead, was clearly much on their minds.

Coming to Black Mountain the spring of 1954 was equally gain of that *viability* in writing without which it, of necessity, atrophies and becomes a literature merely. Robert Duncan, in recent conversation, recalled his own intention then, "to transform American literature into a viable *language*—that's what we were trying to do . . ." Speaking of Frank O'Hara, he noted that extraordinary poet's attempt "to keep the *demand* on the language as *operative,* so that something was at issue all the time, and, at the same time, to make it almost like chatter on the telephone that nobody was going to pay attention to before . . . that the language gain what was assumed before to be its *trivial* uses.

I'm sort of fascinated that *trivial* means the same thing as *three* (Hecate). Trivial's the *crisis,* where it always blows. So I think that one can build a picture, that in all the arts, especially in America, they are *operative.* We think of art as doing something, taking hold of it as a *process . . .*"

At Black Mountain these preoccupations were insistent. For the painters, the information centered in the work of the Abstract Expressionists, many of whom had been either visitors or teachers there—although their large public approval was yet to come. What fascinated me was that they were entirely centered upon the requalification of the *occasion* of painting or sculpture, the sense of what it was given to *do.* Again, a *literature,* in this case art history and criticism, had grown over the viable condition of the possibility. So, as John Chamberlain put it, "a sculpture is something that if it falls on your foot it will break it," both foot and sculpture. It weighs a lot. It sits on a so-called pediment. In contrast, he wanted a new vocabulary to speak of what a sculpture might be, terms like "fluff" or "glare." When asked why he had used discarded automobile parts for much of his early work, his answer was that Michelangelo had had, apparently, a lot of marble sitting in his backyard, but junked automobiles were what Chamberlain found in his own. *Material* was crucial again, regaining the tensions, the instant-to-instant recognition of the nature of what *was* in hand as mind took hold of it. In contrast, John Altoon saw the School of Paris as so much "polishing of stones," what R.B. Kitaj calls a "patinazation," a concern with decorative texture which prevented perception of the possibilities of the *act* of painting itself.

In like sense, *all* assumptions of what a painting was were being intensively requalified. Hence the lovely definition of that time: *a painting is a two-dimensional surface more or less covered with paint.* Williams' definition of a poem is parallel: *a large or small machine made of words.* In each case there is the marked attempt to be rid of the overlay of a speciously 'historical' 'appreciation,' a 'tradition' which is finally nothing more than congealed 'taste' or 'style'—which, Duncan notes, is distinctly different from art. "No man needs an art unless he himself has to put things together—to find an equilibration . . ." Style is predicated on the habit of discrimination previous to experience of the objects thus defined, whether these be so-called "art objects" or simply the clutter of a dump or city street. Duncan's point is that "the objects are not arriving [in perception or consciousness] that way, nor are the objects of thought arriving that way . . ." The collage or assemblage art of Wallace Berman, George Herms, and Larry Jordan—all working in San Francisco in the fifties—makes use of a *conglomerate,* coming out of what people discard, out of *any* time.

Possibly the attraction the artist had for people like myself—think of O'Hara, Ashbery, Koch, Duncan, McClure, Ginsberg; or Kerouac's wistful claim that he could probably paint better than Kline—was that lovely, uncluttered directness of perception and act we found in so many of them. I sat for hours on end listening to Franz Kline in the Cedar Bar, fascinated by, literally, all that he had to say. I can remember the endless variations he and Earl Kerkham spun on the "It only hurts when I smile" saga, and if that wasn't instance of initial story telling (an *art*), I don't think I'll ever know what is or can be. Kline could locate the most articulate senses of human reality in seemingly casual conversation—as I remember he once did, painfully, moving, by means of the *flowers* in a flower shop a friend had just opened to the *roses* Kline had once brought to the pier to welcome his bride from England—to find that she had had a breakdown in passage. Those "flowers" gave us both something to hold on to.

It may also have been the *energy* these people generated, which so attracted us, and we may have been there simply to rip it off in a manner Wyndham Lewis warned against long ago. Writers have the true complication of using words as initial material and then depending on them as well for a more reflective agency. It would be absurd to qualify artists as non-verbal if, by that term, one meant they lacked a generative vocabulary wherewith to articulate their so-called feelings and perceptions. The subtlety with which they qualified the possibility of *gesture* was dazzling. So Michael McClure speaks of having "totally bought Abstract Expressionism as spiritual autobiography" and of Pollock as "so integral [to his own life and thought] that his work began immersing my way of thinking in such a subtle way so early I can't tell you when . . ."

The insistent preoccupation among writers of the company I shared was, as Olson puts it in his key essay, "Projective Verse" (1950): "what is the process by which a poet gets in, at all points energy at least the equivalent of the energy which propelled him in the first place, yet an energy which is peculiar to verse alone and which will be, obviously, also different from the energy which the reader, because he is a third term, will take away?" Duncan recalls that painters of his interest were already "trying to have something *happen* in painting" and that painting was "moving away from the inertness of its being on walls and being looked *at . . ." Action* painting was the term that fascinated him, and questions such as "to what degree was Still an Action painter?" He recognized "that you see the energy back of the brush as much as you see color, it's as evident and that's what you experience when you're looking." He notes the parallel with his work of this time, "The Venice Poem," which is "shaped by its own energies" rather than by a dependence on the pictorial or descriptive. Most emphatically, it is "not shaped to carry something outside of itself."

In his *Autobiography,* published in 1951, Williams reprints the opening section of "Projective Verse," feeling it "an advance of estimable proportions" insofar as Olson was "looking at the poems as a field rather than an assembly of more or less ankylosed lines." Earlier, seeing the text in manuscript, he had responded enthusiastically, noting that "Everything leans on the verb." *Energy* and *field* are insistently in mind in his attempt to desentimentalize accumulated senses of poetry by asserting its *thingness*. He uses his friend, the painter Charles Sheeler, as context: "The poem (in Charles's case the painting) is the construction in understandable limits of his life. That is Sheeler; that, lucky for him, partial or possible, is also music. It is called also a marriage. All these terms have to be redefined, a marriage has to be seen as a thing. The poem is made of things—on a field."

This necessity—to regain a focus not overlaid with habits of *taste* and the *conveniences* of the past—is found in all the arts at this time. At a retrospective show of his early work (in company with Claes Oldenburg and George Segal) Jim Dine said it constituted his own battle with 'art history,' his specific attempt to test and find alternatives for its assumptions. In like sense I once heard John Cage, speaking to a group of hostile and 'classically' oriented music majors at a New York university, point out that the music with which they were engaged had to do with *concept* and its understanding, whereas the music to which he was committed had to do with *perception* and its arousal. He also made the point that their music occupied only one fourth of the spectrum from a theoretic silence to white noise. Being an American, as he said, he felt that wasteful, and was also particularly interested in the possibilities of what's called *noise* itself. Just as Williams had to fight all his life the curious stigma which labelled him "antipoetic" (a term unintentionally provided by Wallace Stevens in an early review of his work, which Stevens wanted to separate from saccharine notions of poetry), so we had to fight to gain a specific diction common to lives then being lived. No doubt the implicit *energy* of such language was itself attractive, but the arguments against it, coming primarily from the then powerful New Critics, made its use an exhausting battle. Allen Ginsberg remembers coming offstage after his early readings of *Howl* often so nervously worn out and shocked by the public antagonism, that he'd go to the nearest toilet to vomit. In contrast—and in grotesque parallel indeed to what was the literal condition of the 'world'—we both remembered the authoritative critical works of the time we were in college, books with titles like *The Rage for Order* and *The Well Wrought Urn.* Whatever was meant by *The Armed Vision,* the guns were seemingly pointed at us.

There was also the idea, call it, that poets as Ginsberg or myself were incapable of the formal clarities that poetry, in one way or another, has obviously to do with. Even now, at public readings in which I've read a sequence of poems whose structure has persistently to do with the parallel *sounds* of words having marked recurrence, someone inevitably (and too often one of my colleagues in teaching) will ask me if I've ever considered using rhyme? It blows my mind! I can't for the life of me figure out *where* they are in so-called time and space. As Pound pointed out, we don't all of us occupy the same *experience* of those situations, no matter we may be alive together in the same moment and place.

When my first wife and I decided at last to separate in 1955, we met in New York to discuss the sad responsibilities of that fact. At one point, locked in our argument, I remember we were walking along Eighth Street not far from the Cedar Bar, and suddenly there was Philip Guston, across the street, waving to us. My wife had not met him, and I had but recently, thanks to Kline—and had found him a deeply generous and articulate man. Most flattering was the fact he knew my work, although at that time it would have been hard to find it in any easily public condition. (It's worth noting that De Kooning, Kline, and Guston—the three I knew best—were all of them 'well read,' to put it mildly, and seemingly kept up with the new work of that time as actively as the writers themselves. Guston especially had a great range of 'literary interest.' A poem in *For Love* called "After Mallarmé" is actually a translation of a poem of Jouvet's which Guston quoted to me, having brought me up to his loft, with characteristic kindness, to show me the few paintings still there just previous to his first show with Sidney Janis. My 'translation' is what I could make of the French he quoted, in my scattered recollection of it.) In any case, my wife had become increasingly suspicious of what she felt were the true incompetences of my various heroes, i.e., Kline painted the way he did because he couldn't draw, and Williams wrote in his fashion, because he couldn't rhyme. So here was one she could physically confront, and she didn't waste any time about it. Guston had brought us to a restaurant which had just opened, and so there were free *hors d'oeuvres*—to his and my delight. Once we were seated, she let him have it: *how do you know when a painting is finished* (painting the way you do). He answered very openly and clearly. Given the field of the painting, so to speak, given what might energize it as mass, line, color *et al.*—when he came to that point where any further act would be experienced as a diminishment of that tension (when there was nothing more to *do*, in short), that was when he felt the painting was finished. She let the matter rest, but I knew she felt almost complacently dissatisfied. "He doesn't know what he is doing—he's just fooling around." She, like so many others then and now, did feel that there must be an intention factually outside the work itself, something to be symbolized there, some content elsewise in mind there expressed, as they say. But that a *process*—again to emphasize it—might be felt and acted upon as crucial in itself she had not considered. So a statement such as Olson's "We do what we know before we know what we do" would be only a meaningless conundrum at best. I guess she thought we were all dumb.

Far from it, for whatever use it proved. There was, first of all, a dearly held to sense of one's *professionalism*, as Duncan reminded me, and all of us *practiced* the art which involved us as best we could. He spoke of the "upsurge in the comprehension of the language" in each art, and "not only writing, or painting, was going on, but *reading*," a veritable checking out of all the possibilities inherent in the physical situation and associative values pertaining. So painters are working "from a very solid comprehension of the visual language they come from, including anyone who may be looking." They know, as do the poets related, the *state* of the language—in a sense parallel to the scientist's saying something is in a volatile or inert *state*—so that "we do convey what we mean" and there is attention to what is happening in *every* part of the work, to keep "a tension throughout."

The diversity of possibilities gained by such an intensive inquiry is still the dominant condition. At times it may seem almost too large an invitation to accept, and in any situation where it is used either for convenience or habit, an expectable bag of tricks, then whatever it may have generated is at an end. This is to say, more vaguely, what Ezra Pound emphasized: "You cannot have literature without *curiosity* . . ." Or what Olson's qualification of *attention* makes clear: "the exaction must be so complete, that the assurance of the ear is purchased at the highest—forty-hour-a-day—price . . ." There is also the dilemma demonstrated by the story Chamberlain tells of his first wife: "She said she wanted to be a singer, but what she really wanted to be was famous." Good luck.

Possibly the complex of circumstances which made the years 1950 to 1965 so decisive in the arts will not easily recur. No one can make it up, so to speak. But there were clearly years before, equally decisive, and there will no doubt be those now after. This clothesline is at best an invention of pseudo-history, and the arts do not intend to be history in this way, however much they use the traditions intimate to their practice. When Duncan saw Olson for the last time, in hospital a few days before his death, he said to him, "important as history was to you, there are no followers—and as a matter of fact that isn't what happened in poetry." Olson grinned, and Duncan added, "It *was* an adventure . . ."

It's always an *adventure,* thank god. When Rauschenberg

arrived at the Art Students League in New York, one of his teachers, Morris Kantor, felt that his wife, who'd come with him, really had the more practical competence as a painter. But what Rauschenberg had as curiosity was fascinating, e.g., he'd put a large piece of butcher paper just in front of the door by which students came and went, would leave it there for a day or so, and then would examine it intently, to see the nature of pattern and imprint which had accumulated. Characteristically it is Rauschenberg who questions that an 'art object' should live forever necessarily, or that it should be less valued than a car which manages to stay in pristine state for a very few years indeed.

What seems most to have been in mind was not the making of *models,* nor some hope of saving a world. As Duncan said of Olson's sense of a city, "You have to confront it and get with it," not "straighten it out. Optimism and pessimism have nothing to do with being alive." The question more aptly is, "How much aliveness is found in living in a city," as much to the point now as when Whitman made his own extraordinary catalog. Moral as the arts are in their literal practice, I do think they abjure such program in other respects. At least they do not serve easily such confined attention, however humanly good. I am sure Allen Ginsberg, despite the persistent concern he has shown for the moral state of this country, would nonetheless yield all for that moment of consciousness which might transform him.

But none of this, finally, has anything to do with any such argument at all. As Wittgenstein charmingly says, "A point in space is a place for an argument." You'll have to tell mother we're still on the road.

Placitas, N.M.
August 28, 1974

Last Night

Random Thoughts on San Francisco, March-June 1956

There are lovely moments in the world when persons and place 'burn with a like heat,' as Olson would say. Who knows why, finally, except that some intuition or habit or simply coincidence has arranged that this shall be the case— and all those to be blessed, truly, will be present.

I felt that way, arriving in San Francisco in March of 1956. The city was humanly so beautiful, but that fact would not have changed my mind in itself. I'd left Black Mountain just at the turn of the year, in real despair, with a marriage finally ended, separated from my three children, very confused as to how to support myself—and so I had headed west, for the first time, thinking to be rid of all the 'easternisms' of my New England upbringing and habit. I had friends living in New Mexico—a phenomenal *place* in its own right—and thought to settle there, but after a month or so I found myself restless, dependent, and in no sense clearer as to what might be my next move. An old friend and student from Black Mountain, Ed Dorn, was living in San Francisco, so that's where I headed—to see the Pacific Ocean, if nothing else.

I got there mid-afternoon, if I remember correctly. Ed

and Helene gave me a whirlwind tour of the city, in their tiny Morris Minor, and we drank a lot in celebration. Ed told me that Rexroth had generously invited us to dinner but that he had to go to work at the Greyhound Bus Terminal at six. I in the meantime was getting drunker and drunker, and recall vomiting heavily in the street before going up to Rexroth's apartment. People had already eaten, but tactfully made no point of my late arrival. Later that same night, returning to the Dorns' apartment, I was charmed by the arrival of Allen Ginsberg at midnight (he got off work at the Greyhound Terminal at that hour) and we talked much of the night about writing and "Projective Verse" and his own interest in Kerouac and Burroughs. My information of the former was meager, but fascinating, i.e., Robert Duncan had told me that Kerouac was the man who had written a thousand pages in which the only apparent *physical* action was a neon sign, over a storefront, flashing off and on. Burroughs, in a story that had him confused with Jack, was said to have been asked at a party to demonstrate his expertise with revolvers by shooting an apple off the head of his wife. A gun was given him, he took aim and fired—and sadly killed her. His apocryphal remark was: I should never have used a 45. They always undershoot . . .

Rexroth's weekly *evenings* proved an intensive meeting ground. The Place, a great bar with genial host Leo and sometime bartender John Ryan, was another. One night Allen asked the Dorns and myself to meet him there after he got off work, so he could introduce us to Jack Kerouac, now back in the city. We got there early, and sat at a small table in the front of that small space—and waited, peering about to try to figure out which one of the others might be Jack. I was particularly drawn to a man who was sitting up against the back wall, on the way to the toilet, seemingly alone, sort of musing, with extraordinary eyes and a head that had somehow larger than 'life size' intensity. When Allen came in, he asked us if we'd seen Jack, and we said, no —and then he pointed to this man I'd been watching, and said, there he is. But we had little conversation that night, unhappily. Jack was pretty comatose from drinking, and when we all got back to the apartment he was sharing with Al Sublette to eat—the large steak, I remember, kept getting dropped on the floor in the process of being cooked —Jack passed out on a bed, and when I was delegated to wake him up, he regarded me with those extraordinary eyes and I felt like a didactic idiot.

Remembering now, it all tends to swirl. Great parties at Locke McCorkle's house out in Mill Valley—Allen and Peter charmingly dancing naked among a dense pack of clothed bodies, flowers at the prom! Jack and I sitting on the sidelines, shy, banging on upended pots and pans, 'keeping the beat.' Gary Snyder's wise old-young eyes, his centeredness and shyness also. Phil Whalen's, "Well, Creeley, I *hope* you know what you're doing . . ." Visits to Mike McClure's with Ed—Ronnie Bladen upstairs in their undesignated commune. Mike practicing the trumpet (in the cellar?)—anyhow, blasts of sound, and talk of Pollock, *energy.* Lawrence Ferlinghetti, standing outside his great and initial City Lights Bookstore, asking me what living was like in Mallorca—cheap? He'd had the care to review *The Gold Diggers* for the *San Francisco Chronicle*, and that was surely a first. Walking around the city with Allen and Phil, Allen reading us *Howl*, which he had in a big black binder notebook, each time we'd stop at a curb or in a cafe (Mike's— great Italian food) or just on a bench in a park. Later I typed the stencils for a small 'edition' of that transforming poem—I was trying to get work and Martha Rexroth gave me the job, as I remember, Allen had given her—prior to the City Lights publication.

There were other dear friends of that time, James Broughton (an old friend of Duncan's), Kermit Sheets, Madeline Gleason. (Duncan himself was in Black Mountain, but his care that I should be at home in the city was so kind.) I'd go to them when I was exhausted, and that was frequently. I finally managed to get an apartment on Montgomery Street, though I never succeeded in living there. I did write some poems, though—on a huge typewiter Martha had got me: "Please," "The Bed," "Just Friends" (old Charlie Parker favorite), "She Went to Stay," "A Folk Song," and "Jack's Blues" among them. One night I invited the gang over, like they say, and one of the company was a particularly ominous *heavy,* whose pleasure was turning school girls on (there were two with him) to heroin, and finally I got freaked. Peter Orlovsky, true angel, somehow managed to clear the whole room of people, then paused himself at the door before leaving, to say, would you like me to turn off the light?

We talked endlessly, day and night. We rehearsed our senses of writing, possible publication, shop talk. Jack was *not* going to let the editors cut up *On The Road* the way they had *The Town and the City*—he was getting himself ready for Malcolm Cowley's impending visit, 'to talk it over,' which Jack rightly feared might be heavy-handed 'advice.' Both Ed and I were asked a lot of questions about Olson and his "Projective Verse"—was it just more razzle-dazzle intellectualism? McClure and Whalen were particularly intrigued, and were at this time already in correspondence with him. Allen, as always, was alert to any information of *process* that might be of use.

So time went by—and it was so packed with things *happening,* it seems now strange to me it was such a short time—only three months. Came June, and I was restless again, and so headed back to New Mexico, with huge rucksack (I managed to get all my stuff *and* Martha's typewriter into somehow) and sleeping bag Jack had helped me locate in an army surplus store on Market Street. I still have them. The sleeping bag, in fact, is presently on the bed in the next room.

Why does that matter. At times it seems all we have of the human possibility, *to keep the faith*—though why an old sleeping bag and a primordial army issue rucksack now looking like a faded grey ghost should be the tokens,

one must figure for oneself. Each time I drive cross country, in the underpowered battered VW I likewise hold on to,
hitting those Kansas spaces (where Burroughs rightly remarked, one gets the *fear*), I think of Neal Cassady and that
Pontiac he could wheel round corners as if on a turntable.
Pure burning energy. Listening to fantastic "Bombay Express" Indian record of Locke's, Neal flagging the train on
through . . .

People give you life in that way. Things you didn't
think you knew or could do. Suddenly it's possible. An-
swers you never expected to come out of your own mouth.
One time—after a night-long party at Locke's—people had
variously come to rest either in the house at the bottom of
the hill, great sloping ground of musky eucalyptus and
grass, or else in the small cabin toward the top, kids and
big people all together in one heap—Jack proposed he and I
sleep outside just to dig that wild soft air and tender darkness. I woke in bright dazzling morning light, with Jack's
face inches from mine, asking in mock sternness: *Are you
pure?* To which I replied, as if for that moment in *his*
mind, *that's like asking water to be wet.*

Buffalo, N.Y.
September 13, 1974

90

Here

What is a play.
A play is scenery.
A play is not identity or place
or time but it like to feel it oh yes
it does wonderfully like to feel it.
That is what makes it a play.

—Gertrude Stein, *The Geographical History of America*

"A play is scenery." In a lecture ("Plays," 1934) she speaks of a play as being *a landscape.* In either case the usual process of familiarizing oneself with casual patterns of identity, or of place or time, the "progressive familiarity" one gains in reading a novel, is absent—"the actors are there they are there and they are there right away." That, as she says, has "a great deal to do with the nervousness of the theatre excitement," insofar as "the introduction to the characters on the stage has a great many different sides to it." Then there is the fact of her "early recollections . . . One which is in a way like a circus that is the general movement and light and air which any theatre has, and a great deal of glitter in the light and a great deal of height in the air, and then there are moments, a very very few moments but still moments. One must be pretty far advanced in adolescence before one realizes a whole play."

A little later in the same lecture she speaks very movingly of being adolescent "and going to the theatre all the time, a great deal alone, and all of it making an outside inside existence for me, not so real as books, which were all inside me, but so real that it the theatre made real outside me which up to that time I never had been in my emotion. I had largely been so in an active daily life but not in any emotion." The problem then met with, sadly, was, "the great difficulty of having my emotion accompany the scene and then moreover I became fairly consciously troubled by the things over which one stumbles over which one stumbled to such an extent that the time of one's emotions in relation to the scene was always interrupted . . . Could I see and hear and feel at the same time and did I." What then comes as solution is Sarah Bernhardt—"it was all so foreign and her voice being so varied and it all being so french I could rest in it untroubled. And I did . . . This experience curiously enough and yet perhaps it was not so curious awakened in me a desire for melodrama on the stage, because there again everything happened so quietly one did not have to get acquainted and as what the people felt was of no importance one did not have to realize what was said."

These several statements are most interesting to me, just that they locate very clearly her own preoccupations— the possible situations of *time,* specifically the nature of the *present* as interior and exterior condition—and the experiential location, so to speak, which the stage *per se* had to offer. One sturdy fact of existence would seem to me at least that whatever *happens* in the world, or can be said to have happened or to be about to happen, or eventually, is, by nature of the necessity constituted by the statement itself, happening *now.* There seemingly is no other 'place' for it to occur. Of course there are endlessly possible patterns of causality, most usefully so very often, but their reality also is dependent on this specific *now* insofar as they presume a precedent or a consequence for what it is (*now*) they are involved with.

Thinking of a "play" and "scenery" and "landscape" (and *not* of "identity" and "place" and "time," for these are abstractions which accumulate their various meanings rather than possess them by fact of activity or literal substance), all three have the common quality of being primarily a *present* event. Their significance takes root in their being 'here and now' and their history or consequence seems secondary, despite its possible relevance. In like sense, *feeling*, as one says, is insistently a present reality. It may be useless to "cry over spilt milk" but feeling will never know it, only thought. And thought itself may be issue, finally, of feeling. Thus "it likes to feel it oh yes it does wonderfully like to feel it . . . ."

In any case, a disjunct can occur in experience when the "inside" existence of any one of us confronts an existing "outside" which is not in phase or 'in time' with our own. The feeling then of dislocation is very unhappy and, understandably, we avoid such circumstance if we can. Reading, the solution is quite simple. We can put the book down despite its already having 'got into' us, and hopefully, reassert our own experiences of 'place' and 'time' and 'identity,' our so-called various 'selves.'

So there is, put mildly, extraordinary power in any *present* moment, the more so feelings have been powerfully engaged—and by "power" I mean some common sense of *energy*, presumably a basic quantity in activity of whatever order. Something's *happening*. I'm attracted by the fact that Gertrude Stein's qualification of literature was, is it or isn't it *exciting*. It's much like Pound's sense of poetry being language *charged* to the highest degree of that possibility.

Coming to the opera (physically, or in mind), it is, as an activity, *here* and also apparently dominant in relation to any one of us *here* as well. That is, if I get up and start shouting that its activity is not congruent with my own, I'll either find myself flooded with a 'present' equal to my own —thus I'll be *on stage*, intentionally or not *in the act*—or else ejected, much as food is by a preoccupied body. I don't think this has to do with a social fact, in the sense of manners. Rather, it seems the situation of reality itself, which the stage *is*, in its occupation of the common *present*, and the divers alternatives to that situation which each of us in our own particulars might constitute are not so much yielded as enclosed by the power of that event, that *present* which theater in all of its modes—music, dance, drama, or their combination—so particularly creates.

It's all a long way round to come to some rather simple point no doubt. But this *present* is such a true one, gift or given—and she spent her whole life, one might say, insistent upon the nature and condition of its reality. Words. Now. Here. In thought, at least, *there* would be so much more commodious. But, as a sister poet said, *if we're going to be here, let's be here now!*

The Mother of Us All is her last work, makes use of narrative (which her earlier collaboration with Virgil Thomson, *Four Saints in Three Acts,* did not), has personages anachronistically in the same 'time' and 'place,' muses, wisely, on various circumstances of this life (men, marriage, names, women), uses a lifelong acquisition of language's patterns, 'simply' 'elemental':

> Where is where. In my long life of effort and strife, dear life, life is strife, in my long life, it will not come and go, I tell you so, it will stay it will pay but
>
> (A long silence)
>
> But do I want what we have got, has it not gone, what made it live, has it not gone because now it is had, in my long life in my long life
>
> (Silence)
>
> Life is strife, I was a martyr all my life not to what I won but to what was done.
>
> (Silence)
>
> Do you know because I tell you so, or do you know, do you know.
>
> (Silence)

My long life, my long life.

Curtain

Buffalo, N.Y.
September 26, 1975

For Michael

Homage to Michael McClure is both pleasure and duty, in that his work has been a provocation and delight, lo! these (almost) twenty years. First meeting recalled now effortlessly, like they say. I'd crashed on the Dorns in San Francisco circa March 1956, and soon after was taken over to the McClure household, shared in commune manner with divers others, including Jim Harmon and Ronald Bladen. Intensive, physically articulate young man, level voice, eyes remarkably clear and crystalline, viz as with diamonds a cool *light*. Already *going about his business* with undistracted singularity. At one point asks me, generously, if I'd like to go with him to Vic Tanney's (where he worked as an instructor) to *work out*—which scared me, first, that I'd have to *expose* my distraught carcass to possibly pitiless glares and, second, that I might get hurt! Ah well . . .

Fact is Michael's attention is *merciless,* in the sense nothing distracts his mind from body signals pulsing that complicated grey pulp to insights truly *in there*. Talking with him this summer about painting and all in the fifties, he made an interesting emphasis on *value* of "action as an extension of the individual," not otherwise important in itself—in

short, a "meatly" *process.* Unlike contemporaries interested
in cleaning up the dump, I think his persistent involvement
with *meat package* context of persons is to figure the instruction and wherewithal to bring by-product mind-thought
abstractions back home to initial flesh and blood. He's not
ransacking biology, say, for metaphors, nor is he trying to
dream a dream, etc. He's practical, and, artist that is he, he
wants it all, and so "The function of art is not pleasure or
education but to make an extension—a means toward huge-
ness and liberation for the man, the Beast, that invents it
. . . (*Dark Brown,* 1961)."

Fascinating early continuities, i.e., preoccupation with
gesture begins, as he told me, in highschool, where first concerns were natural history and anthropology, moving (with
significant buddy Bruce Connor) then to Dada and Surreal-
ist art—and then to poetry. Struck by painters of the Kootz
Gallery, the Intrasubjectivists, as they were then called:
Tomlin, Motherwell, Stamos, Baziotes, Gottlieb—"biomor-
phic"—and Toby and Graves, out of Surrealism. Motherwell
particularly useful—"an intellective kinship," as he called it.
Then Pollock—"so integral that his work began immersing
my way of thinking in such a subtle way so early I can't
tell you when . . ." "Totally bought Abstract Expressionist
spiritual autobiography . . ." Still and Rothko—with whom
he hoped to study at the San Francisco Art Institute, but
on arrival found they'd just left, so goes to S. F. State
(where daughter Jane has just this fall begun as student:
"Biology/ French I/ Dance/ Blake").

I've been fascinated by the *range* of his statement, i.e.,
the diversity of modes in which he gains means of language.
Sitting with him in empty Fillmore Ballroom watching dress
rehearsal of *The Beard* mid-sixties, just dazzled. Ask him
how he *wrote* this extraordinary play—answer is he copied
down words of the two people speaking in his head, con-
joining to make poles positive: "Meat/Spirit." Wow. Or his
novels, e.g., *The Adept*—where he defines mind-flash subjective state of *invisibility,* just like that. One time when visit-

ing in New Mexico, he got me to read some of the *Ghost Tantras* so that I could *feel* the body resonances and not just skate on the 'meaning.' Poem on postcard he thoughtfully sent another time when my 'world' was 'demonic' beyond belief. (He and Joanna would come out for visit, we'd go down to beach where J/ would wisely go swimming— while the 'gang' packed into Gossip's Corner would be well on way to Ultimate Energy for the evening. As my own eye would begin to glitter, Mike would back off and gracefully split for the city. Just too much too minded too destructively zapped head-tripping wanted the world to narrow to a match flare.)

FOR BOB

EACH
MAMMAL
does
a
small perfect
thing
like
to be himself
or herself
and to hold a new creation
on a shining platter
as he
(or she)
steps toward
the waiting car

"Or how we got drunk & rolled down hills in San Diego or the vision of Spider Rabbit at Kent State . . ." *Dear Friend, this is only the beginning . . .*

Was That a Real Poem
or Did You Just
Make It up Yourself?

As I get older, I recognize that my thinking about poetry may or may not have anything actively to do with my actual work as a poet. This strikes me as no thing cynically awry, but rather seems again instance of that hapless or possibly happy fact, we do not as humans seem necessarily aware of what we are physically or psychically doing at all. One thing, therefore, that does stay put in my head, as something said in youth, is "we live as we can, each day another—there is no use in counting. Nor more, say, to live than what there is, to live. . . ." I did not feel that a pessimistically argued reality back then, nor do I now. It is very hard for me to live in any projection of reality, in a plan or arrangement of the present moment that uses it primarily as a 'future' term. I have long experience of my own restlessness and impatience, and have managed quiet and a feeling of centeredness only when the *here and now* literally discovered it for me. Elsewise I have battered myself and the surroundings with seemingly useless energy, pleased only that something at least was 'happening.'

My writing seems to me no different. Of course I learned as much as I could about the *how* of its occasion.

Like many of my contemporaries I felt myself obliged to be an explicit craftsman so as to have defense against the authoritative poetry of my youth—whose persons I'd like now not to recall just that it's taken me so long to forget them. So, from that initial, crotchety purview, I've continued, finding and choosing as heroes men and women who must at this point be familiar to anyone who has read me at all: Williams, Pound, H.D., Stein, Zukofsky, Olson, Duncan, Levertov, Ginsberg, Dorn, Bunting, Wieners, McClure, Whalen, Snyder, Berrigan—and so on, being those I can almost see out the window if I look. Put more simply, there's been a way of doing things which found company with others, and in that company one has found a particular life of insistent and sustaining kind.

That has been part of the situation of 'what poetry means to me,' but dear as it is, it has not been either the largest part nor the most significant. A few months ago I was sitting with friends in a lovely house on a lovely afternoon, and we began a collaborative poem, on impulse, using an electric typewriter that was on a nearby table. It took me real time to get to it because it intimidated me— I've never used one particularly—and also intrigued me, and so my feelings and thoughts began to singularize me, isolate me in relation to the others. But I've always been able to do that, so to speak. But is it some necessity of my own working? In any case, my contribution to the poem stood painfully clear in its twisted, compressed statement—even the spacing of lines shrank to a small fist of words, defensive and altogether by itself.

No wonder that I've never forgotten Williams' contention that "the poet thinks with his poem, in that lies his thought, and that in itself is the profundity . . ." Poems have always had this nature of revelation for me, becoming apparently objective manifestations of feelings and thoughts otherwise inaccessible. Did I love Mary—a poem or story would quite usually make the answer clear, no matter it might take years to know it. A pleasant woman met this spring pointed out, for example, that "For love—I would/ split open your head and put/ a candle in/ behind the eyes . . ." was a literally violent proposal that was not demonstrably involved with usual senses of 'loving' the recipient. Yet I had always felt that poem a true measure of an ability to love, and possibly it is.

As a young man, then, moved by poetry, feeling its possibilities as inclusive, bringing all the world to one instant of otherwise meaningless 'time,' I wanted, not unexpectedly, to participate in that wonder. We struggle with them a good deal, mutter, mistake, but *words* seem even so significantly common and in that respect accessible. My own commitment to them was not easily understood. Was it that nothing else was open to me? Did I turn to them simply that no other act or substance permitted me such occasion? I know that I felt in those years now past very often useless in other attempts to find place in the world. As so many of that time, I married primarily to reify what might be called my existence. The fact of wanting to be a social person, as well as a private one, seemingly demanded it. Again, there was nothing I otherwise 'did' that argued my relevance to a general world.

In short, I was markedly self-preoccupied, lonely, inarticulate at crucial points in my relationships, and again, and again, restless. If they did nothing else, words gave instant reality to this insistent flux, which otherwise blurred, faded, was gone before another might in any sense witness it. That poems, stories, fed on this experience of reality was of great use initially. Just as I had used reading as a place to be, a world of volatile and active nature yet also 'unreal,' not 'flesh and blood'—and yet that surely, how else could it be —so now the possibilities that words might engender became a deep preoccupation.

At various times I've put emphasis on the fact that I was raised in New England, in Massachusetts for the most part. So placing myself, I've argued that that fact clarifies my apparently laconic way of saying things, expecially so in my early poems. But might that use of words not come also of feeling tentative with them, unsure of their appropriate significations—as though there were a *right* way that was being distorted, lost, by fact of one's ignorance? I sense an aspect of this dilemma in Williams' plaint, "many years of reading have not made you wise. . . ." I know that he did share with me a tacit fear of the well-trained, academically secure *good English* he felt the comfortable equipment of various of his contemporaries. We both depended, it would seem, on enthusiasms, rushes of insight or impulse, read only to a purpose if the appetite underlying would settle for nothing else. I was delighted, for example, to realize that Williams did not spend long hours researching *Paterson* in the library but rather, as Michael Weaver first told me, got his information from a lovely, old time *local* historian. To this day I am so intimidated by the *nature* of libraries, the feel of them, the authority of their ordering of books on shelves, etc., that I rarely if ever go into them. I feel toward them much as I feel toward telephones, that their function is disastrously limited by their form, no matter what efficiencies are also clearly the case.

But why worry about that? If one has spent close to thirty years writing books, in effect, why be so fearful of this one place they may come to rest? Why be afraid of *poems,* for that matter? Thinking of that world 'out there,' and recalling my own tentativeness in trying to find my own use in it, always the *general* measure of reality can hurt me, can say, in short, 'of course *you* like it, you wrote it—but what about other people, don't you care what they think or feel or want?' More specifically, why not write poems the way they are supposed to be written—as simple acquaintance with poetry as a *subject* would easily define. Thus, if you seriously want to be a poet, you study the prevailing models of its activity and you set yourself to their imitation as diligently as you can. And slowly you acquire, or do not, the requisite ability.

I don't believe it. I *know* that attention to what has

been written, what is being written, is a dearly rewarding experience. Nonetheless, it is *not* the primary fact. Far closer would be having a horse, say, however nebulous or lumpy, and, seeing other people with horses, using their occasion with said horses as some instance of the possibility involved. In short, I would never buy a horse or write a poem simply that others had done so—although I would go swimming on those terms or eat snails. Stuck with the horse, or blessed with it, I have to work out that relation as best I can.

Posit that music exists despite the possibility that no one might be consciously able to make it, that what we call *poems* are an intrinsic fact in the human world whether or no there be poets at this moment capable of their creation. That would characterize my belief—which gives me no rest, which, too often, causes a despairing sense of uselessness and ineptitude. Why can't *I* write them, fall in love, reveal the actual world, and be the hero in it? Isn't it *mine*. No. Yours? No. Theirs? No. Ours? No.

Days, weeks, months and sometimes years can pass in that sad place. Nothing gets done, nothing really gets even started. A vague, persistent echo of possibility seems all that is there to depend upon. Perhaps tomorrow, or later today—or even right now. To work. Useless paper, useless pen. Scribbles of habit and egocentric dependence. But you did it once, didn't you—they said so, you thought so too. Try again.

Sometime in the mid-sixties I grew inexorably bored with the tidy containment of clusters of words on single pieces of paper called 'poems'—"this will really get them, wrap it up. . . ." I could see nothing in my life nor those of others adjacent that supported this single hits theory. Dishonest to say I hadn't myself liked it, haiku, for example, or such of my own poems that unwittingly opened like seeds. But my own life, I felt increasingly, was a *continuance,* from wherever it had started to wherever it might end —of course I felt it as linear in time—and here were these quite small *things* I was tossing out from time to time, in the hope that they might survive my own being hauled on toward terminus. Time to start over, afresh, began to be felt at first as increasingly limited, finally as nonexistent. The intensive, singularly made poems of my youth faded as, hopefully, the anguish that was used in the writing of so many of them also did. I was happier? Truly pointless to answer insofar as I lived now in another body and with an altered mind.

More, what specific use to continue the writing of such poems if the need therefore be only the maintenance of some ego state, the so-called *me*-ness of that imaginary person. Lost in some confusion of integrity, I had to tell the truth, however unreal, and persisted toward its realization, even though unthinkable. So writing, in this sense, began to lose its specific edges, its singleness of occurrence, and I worked to be open to the casual, the commonplace, that which collected itself. The world transformed to bits of paper, torn words, 'it/it.' Its continuity became again physical. I had no idea of its purpose, nor mine, more than a need to include all that might so come to mind and survive to be written.

My tidinesses, however, are insistent. Thus forms of things said moved through accumulated habits of order, and I felt neither ease nor possibility in the jumbled or blurred contexts of language. No doubt I will repeat the manners of small kid with mother town nurse and older sister most articulate in West Acton, Mass., 1930 to 1935 forever. Only the town is changed, to protect the innocent.

If one were a musician, the delight might be sounding again and again all that composite of articulation had preceded one, the old songs truly. In poetry, the dilemma of the circumstance is simply that some*one* is supposed to write some*thing,* and it becomes a possessive and distracting point of view. It is interesting to remember that Archilochus and Sappho are known to us because literacy comes to 'write them down,' no necessary concern of theirs nor of lyric poetry more generally. Yet I am very much a person of my time in wanting to leave a record, a composite fact of the experience of living in time and space. It was Charles Olson's hope to make an *image of man* in writing *The Maximus Poems*—not at all to write some autobiographical memoir. I use all poetry to write anything, and only wish I might know more of its vast body, which is seemingly as various as the earth itself.

What *is* poetry? In a dictionary I've hauled around for almost as long as I've been writing (*The Pocket Oxford Dictionary of Current English*, Fowler and Fowler, in a "New and Enlarged Edition revised by George Van Santvoord," 1935), it says to my horror: "elevated expression of elevated thought or feeling, esp. in metrical form. . . ." If I turn to a more recent dictionary, *The American Heritage Dictionary of the English Language*, 1969, I'm told that poetry is "the art or work of a poet," which has got to be a cop-out. So all these years people have been screaming that one was not writing *real* poetry—and it turns out nobody, certainly no one in that crowd, knew what it was to begin with. No wonder they insisted on those *forms*! They wouldn't know it *was* a woman unless she was wearing a dress.

So now I will make up poetry, as I always have, one word after another, becoming something, as sounds, call them, as beats, *tum tum.* All very familiar. But each time I take the bus I do see something new, somehow. Eyes possibly? Certainly a turning world. Verse turns, and takes turns in turning—which are called *verses,* in my book, like changes—and not those *stanzas* or stops, standstills. *Onward then, multiple men, women too, will go with you*—boohoo. Which is a poem because I say so, it *rhymes.* That was a primary requisite for years and years. But so lovely when such rhyming, that congruence of sounds which occur in time with sufficient closeness, to resound, echo, and so recall, when *that* moves to delight and intensity, feeling the physical quality of the words' movement with a grace that distorts nothing. To *say* things—and to say them with such articulation can bring them physical character in the words which have become them—is *wonder*.

It is equal wonder when the rhythms which words can embody move to like echo and congruence. It is a *place*, in short, one has come to, where words dance truly in an information of one another, drawing in the attention, provoking feelings to participate.

Poems have involved an extraordinary range of human and non-human event, so to discuss that fact seems pointless. We will talk of everything sooner or later. Americans have had the especial virtue in the last hundred years of opening both content and form in an extraordinary manner, and the energy inherent continues without apparent end.

But again, one lives a life, and so, personally, one speaks of it, and of the people and places it was given to find. I cannot say that my children particularly respect or find other interest in my being a poet, and, at first, that bothered me because I wanted them moved by what moved me. False hope, I now think—although it might otherwise come to be the case. At times I hear the niggard comment that poets seem only to have other poets as an audience. It is certainly true that the dearest company I've had in reading has been so. But many people otherwise have heard too, through no intent of mine. I couldn't predicate they would, in writing. As a young man I questioned that anyone would ever hear at all, although it did not occur to me that I might therefore stop writing.

The tacit lament in this way of speaking strikes me as pathetic. Getting a purchase on writing, so to speak, was for me a one way ticket to bliss. I've never really come back. In those long, lonely nights I've wailed the sweetest songs, possibly, certainly those most designed for my own pleasure. Years back, again, Williams said, why don't we make clear we write for our pleasure, that we *like* doing it? It's a fair question. Nobody wants their pleasures criticized, and that fact no doubt explains why nobody really wants to be explained, nor wants to explain either. And I suppose that's why one uses either a tendentiously 'critical' vocabulary in speaking of 'his work' or else pushes clear with a, gee whiz, fellers, it's really nothing.

At first I was intent upon getting *anything* to hold, so that the experience in reading had the same qualities as the impulse in writing. But then I don't really know, nor have I ever, what's being said until it comes to some close, and it's now there to be read through, as one thing. Elsewise I trust the location implicit in feeling it's going well, opening, moving without a sense of hesitance or forced intention. I don't want to write what is only an idea, particularly my own. If the world can't come true in that place, flooding all terms of my thought and experience, then it's not enough, either for me or, equally, for anyone else. It must be somehow *revelation,* no matter how modest that transformation can sometimes be. Or vast, truly—"the world in a grain of sand."

The title for these divers thoughts comes from a lovely story told me about 1960 by John Frederick Nims in Chicago as he afforded us a charming lunch in his role as editor of *Poetry.* It concerned a friend of his, another poet, who had been on a tour of readings in the Middle West. And, as was his wont, he invited questions from the audience at one particular college, on completion of his reading. And a guy puts up his hand and says, tell me, that next to last poem you read—was that a real poem or did you just make it up yourself? Terrific. That's stuck in my head so lucently so long! Much as the phenomenon of another friend and student at Black Mountain in the middle fifties, who in truth could perceive no demonstrable difference between a cluster of words called *poem* and a cluster of words called *prose.* She felt the typographical form of the poem was all that apparently defined it—and that of course was a very arbitrary gimmick, to her mind. I tried everything, "Mary had a little lamb," tum te tum, clapped my hands with the beat, pulled out the vowels à la Yeats, probably even sang. Still it stayed flat and arbitrary. She felt the beat and texture of the sound was imposed by will of the reader and was not initial in the words themselves. All the usual critical terms were of course useless, far too abstract. Finally I truly despaired of gaining more than her sympathy and patience. Then one day, we were reading Edward Marshall's "Leave the Word Alone," and for some immaculate and utterly unanticipated "reason" she *got* it, she heard all the play of rhythms and sounds bringing that extraordinary statement of primary humanness into such a density of feeling and song.

Would that all had such a happy ending—and 'American poetry,' like they say, soared on to the stars. Senses of progress, also familiar, really want that in the worst way. Meantime one's brothers and sisters are out there somewhere wailing on, to make the night a little lighter, the day a little brighter, like. Bringing that sun up and bringing it down again, every time. I don't know where it's supposed to 'get to' in that sense, more than to persist in the clarity of human recognitions and wonder. Poetry, as Duncan says, comes "from a well deeper than time." It's 'contemporary' in the way that fire, air, water or earth might be said to be particularly involved in any apprehension of present existence. Sadly it can, as these, go away, be lost to other appetites and acts. Talking to Michael McClure a few days ago, thinking of the primary *stances* in the arts, to the three most familiar (Classicism, Romanticism, and Surrealism) he felt a fourth might be added: the Beat, which, distinct from the other three, does not propose 'the world' as a stable, physical *given* but, in ecological terms, realizes its fragility and thus the need for human attention and care.

As a poet, at this moment—half listening as I am to the House Judiciary Committee's deliberations—I am angered, contemptuous, impatient, and possibly even cynical concerning the situation of our lives in this 'national' place. Language has, publicly, become such an instrument of coercion, persuasion, and deceit. The power thus collected is ugly beyond description—it is truly *evil*. And it will not go away.

Trust to good verses then . . . Trust to the clarity instant in being human, that knows and wants no other place.

Bolinas, California
July 31, 1974

Introduction to
The Manner "Music"
by Charles Reznikoff

A story is an extraordinary human possibility, and people have been making use of its resources no doubt since time, like they say, began. There are, of course, many stories, and many ways of telling each story—many, many variations and points of view and opinions as to what, after all, was the point. *What happened? Well, it was like this* . . . So the story begins, or might, to tell *what happened,* or might have happened, or didn't

One had not known, sadly, that Charles Reznikoff wrote novels. That a man should have such quiet and singular genius so modestly put aside (by himself) is regrettable. So much does shout at us, belligerently claiming attention for its style or its intelligence or its newness, that a story such as this one, so shyly assertive of what it so truly knows, is, humanly, such deep relief and reassurance—that one of us *can* care. The circumstances involved with its writing are briefly summarized by its present publisher, John Martin, as follows:

> I have recently gone through Charles Reznikoff's lifetime accumulation of manuscript, and was thunder-

struck to find a carefully typed, completed novel, which he apparently never mentioned to anyone, or submitted for publication. It was, I think, composed in the early 1950's and is called "The Manner *Music*." It is autobiographical, with one character, the narrator of the story, representing an aspect of Charles himself—the Charles who worked as a drummer, selling ladies' hats, who was disillusioned at trying to find the leisure to write, at getting his poetry accepted, etc. The protagonist of the novel, called Jude Dalsimer, is the Charles who never doubted his worth as a poet and who was determined to live out this destiny regardless of circumstance. A third character in the story, called Paul Pasha, is a portrait of Charles' most faithful friend for many years, who was a successful motion picture producer.

I believe this novel was written in response to a letter William Carlos Williams wrote Charles in the late 1940's, at a time when Charles' career was at low ebb, urging him to continue writing at any cost, and if possible to write a novel . . .

Stories are changed in telling, of course, so this one is not a simple rehearsal of a part of a man's life. There are, in fact, many stories here, "the manner, *music*," an interweaving of a complex of "things" happening, being recalled and told. The plot is an ageless one, the story of two men who have known each other since they were boys. One tells us what he knows of the other's life, as he is witness to it but also as the other tells him of it. Times are reasonably good, then are not, then come to the anticipated disaster. Jude Dalsimer, whose life is the novel's center, will not give up his *music*, which is not a secure means of livelihood as his friend well knows, having himself yielded similar hopes for a more dependable job. But, for Jude, it is the means of transforming all the welter of emotion and event into an articulate form. Neither his wife nor friend, nor anyone else, for that matter, can understand it. But, as his friend finally says:

If Jude had wanted to write music and had not done his best to do so, he might have lived longer and more pleasantly but, as he might have explained, it is as if one enlists in an army or perhaps is drafted: he must fight and may fall but may not desert. Most do, of course. I did, I suppose . . .

However, the bare bones of the plot tell little. As the two meet recurrently, over the years, each time Jude rehearses for his friend the circumstances provoking the music, which he then plays for his patient listener. This "background" can be the hauntingly provocative fact of a dog's having followed him, or a party at the house of his boss, the movie director, Paul Pasha, where the conversation leaps from "subject" to "subject":

All this learning was pleasant to the guests who were covering much time and space with little trouble.

Or it can be, instantly and harshly, full fact of the times:

Then the chairman called on a young German who had escaped from a concentration camp. "I was to speak on the literature now written in exile by the refugees from Germany," he said, and the diners leaned forward to listen, although he spoke English well enough and clearly. "But I cannot talk about any such subject now, for I had an experience today I must tell you about . . ."

Then that story follows, as do others, layer on layer, arriving at no simple point or conclusion, but, instead, gathering into a multiple density of impressions, and impacts, events, of literally common people. The two friends frequently eat together, and there is always an overt calculation of the provision, of the people employed in it, a comparison of its resources as against another's. There is the Jew in the Gentile's world, the explicit or tacit confrontation. There are the successful men and women, and, as the story goes on, the unsuccessful and destitute. There are insistently places, so plainly yet vividly remarked one will never forget them:

> Further on, the lonely street passed the foot of a cliff and suddenly among the boulders, right above a drop of twenty feet or so, a man stood up, face as grey as stone, clothes dark with dirt: he might have been a wild animal that had made its home there, almost indistinguishable among the rocks, and he, too, looked at me. I saw a path, at least a slope, down which he could come if he wanted to and his nerves were good enough. I supposed they were, to stand where he did. But he did not move. The cliff rose above him for a hundred feet or more to the cement foundations that outmeasured the houses themselves. Then he turned and began to pick his way slowly among the rocks along the cliff.

The friend, who is listener and witness, has no exceptional judgment to make. He tells the story as it is told to him, and otherwise recounts his own observations and impressions. One feels that his interest in Jude is fact of old loyalty, and some curiosity to find out, each time there is the possibility, what has become of his old chum. His own life is not primarily involved, nor told, except for the brief information of his selling trips. He has feelings, criticisms at times, but he has nothing to say that will change a thing. His life will go on, certainly, with or without Jude Dalsimer.

How common a situation—someone one used to know. Nothing finally so remarkable about that fact, or any other like it. Certainly nothing heroic in this case. And yet it seems to change everything, with its futility, its despair. Why is he telling me this, one wants to say—as no doubt Jude's patient friend must often have said to himself, or *playing* me this, this *music* I neither like nor understand.

I am afraid, however, that I listened to other of Jude's enthusiams as I listened to his playing—politely but at heart indifferent.

Why can't *that* be understood. And yet—it seems to change everything. Charles Reznikoff's power as a poet, always, and now in this novel, without exception, is his singular ability to state the case—not the right answer, or the wrong one—but the *case*. Put most simply, as he himself does in a manuscript found among his papers at his death in 1976, "First, there is the Need":

> With respect to the treatment of subject matter in verse [or in this novel] and the use of the term "objectivist" and "objectivism," let me again refer to the rules with respect to testimony in a court of law. Evidence to be admissable in a trial cannot state conclusions of fact: it must state the facts themselves. For example, a witness in an action for negligence cannot say: the man injured was negligent in crossing the street. He must limit himself to a description of how the man crossed: did he stop before crossing? Did he look? Did he listen? The conclusions of fact are for the jury and let us add, in our case, for the reader.

San Feliu de Guixols,
Spain, 1977

Ecce Homo

Introduction to Catalog of **R.B. Kitaj** Exhibition,
Marlborough Galleries, London and Zurich, 1977

One evening last year in San Francisco, a number of people came together to hear discussion of a nonhuman concept of *beauty*, e.g., what a butterfly or blue whale or a three-toed sloth might 'define' as beautiful in another member of its group. The zoologist, Peter Warshall, emphasized that it was, seemingly, those functions or physical attributes which permitted the most appropriate (secure and productive) rapport with environment, that were chosen. I was interested that the other participant that evening was Diane di Prima, whose *Revolutionary Letters* constitute a basic 'how-to' manual for social-political survival. The series itself, of which this evening was one instance, had been arranged by the physicist Frank Oppenheimer, who, with his brother, Robert, had faced a severely imposed 'question' as to legal conditions of human interest and commitment during the fifties.

Whether the art be painting, music or writing, one may note its overwhelming preoccupation with *process* during the periods of the Modern and, now, the Post Modern. Also echoing in mind is William Burroughs' somewhat sardonic remark in *The Naked Lunch*, "Where do they go when they leave the body. . . ." One may presume that the substantially collective *human* body was left toward the end of the nineteenth century, and that, in the western world, the faintness of an intellectual humanism, having no physical authority for its ruminations, went down also, as increasingly sophisticated fragmentations of the human event took over. The point here can be made simply by noting some of the primary names of that time, Freud, Einstein, Marx et al.—each of whom, be it said, thought to speak for a collective situation of the human, but, nonetheless, presents primarily a singular plane of its event. *Schizophrenia,* as Surrealism or Cubism, is a term invented about the time of World War I, and Ezra Pound's great cry *de profundis,* "I cannot make it cohere . . .", has obvious parallel with Yeats —"The centre cannot hold. . . ."

What had been lost, to put it so, was an *image of man,* some order of and in experience, both collective and singular, that could propose itself as constituting *something,* in whatever dimension or context of practical fact was elsewise the case. The insistent, whining question of our time is, "Who am I?"—and that *I* is not the one which is of necessity the many, plural and communal as given. Quite the contrary, it is Descartes' proof of existence, swollen with paranoia and frustration to a *me* of irreconcilable abstraction. Marlowe's Faustus—possibly the first significant instance of this crisis in our literature—now becomes Everyman. "O, I'll leap up to my God! Who pulls me down?" Be it said that there are a remarkable number of cultures and persons surviving who do not share in our specifically Western dilemma, but our equally specific use of the world since 1900 has resulted in a horrifying reduction of such cultural units and the language groups relating.

In his notes concerning "The Human Clay," an exhibition he selected for the Arts Council of Great Britain (1976), Kitaj says, with disarming simplicity, "The single human figure is a swell thing to draw . . . I'm talking about skill and imagination that can be *seen to be done.* It is, to my way of thinking and in my own experience, the most difficult thing to do really well in the whole art. . . . It is there that the artist truly 'shows his hand' for me. It is then that I can share in the virtue of failed ambition and the downright revelation of skill. . . ." This preoccupation has nothing to do with a 'documentary' art or with 'photorealism'—each seems too simply an exploitation of a one-sided 'reality.' Rather, it's what that single footprint meant to Robinson Crusoe, in Defoe's mind. It's *there,* physically, without question. What Defoe then realizes, by means of Crusoe, is the *informational* crisis it provokes in another human. So James Joll and John Golding, extraordinary humans indeed, look out 'From London' to see Europe, their own information surrounding—as Kitaj, in turn, sees them, and remembers both the Europe of their insight and his own determining sense of it, all present in such resonant, echoing detail, from such a range of human preoccupation and vocabulary, one cannot simply list its occasions. For one instance, however, see that Mr. Joll's head has been 'repaired' in the manner of certain frescoes of Giotto—which recalls, in turn, that charming Modernist tenet, "a painting is a two-dimensional surface, etc." As Kitaj might say, *of course.*

More complex possibly, as its title, *If Not, Not,* can be felt to signal,* are the multiple dimensions of this painting,

---

* As instance of Kitaj's own social and political context, and the complexity of its resolution here, consider the following from a book found in his library: " 'We who are as good as you swear to you who are no better than we, to accept you as our king, provided you observe all our liberties and laws; but if not, not'—this formula of the ancient coronation oath of Aragon defines the relations of the sovereigns to their noble subjects in all the kingdoms of medieval Spain." F.D. Klingender, *Goya in the Democratic Tradition,* London, 1968 (2nd edition), p. 18. *All* these elements, e.g. Klingender, Goya, etc., can be present, albeit transformed by Kitaj's use of them in the painting itself.

'measures' of an insistent variety of human information and feeling about 'things.' a curious soft welter of 'dreams.' Here the physical order of sight shifts and turns in 'perspective,' informed by diversities of human artifact, presence, and memory. Color leads and coordinates, a deliberating act, insisting on the primacy of the painting as a human decision.

The Jew Etc.—as the earlier Bill—begins a 'character' (like those one might find in a novel, Kitaj said in conversation, who come and go in various possible books) found also in If Not, Not. Here he is singular, in progress—as a 'history' in a shifting 'place.' The other figures thus—as Catalan Christ (Pretending to Be Dead)—are historic increment and prototype, but in situations which have their own decisive echoes and accumulations. The physical dimensions of the 'single figure' paintings themselves are frequently the literal measure of a human space.

If anything stands presently in need of definition, like they say, more demandingly than the word person, I don't myself know what it is or can be. Whether the preoccupations be social, political, psychological, legal, economic, or biological, there seems no commonly satisfying resolution of meaning, either in or among the concepts variously attached. When the zoologist pointed out that particular markings of the Monarch butterfly are apparently considered to be 'beautiful' to others of that species, he presumed that the 'reason' was the camouflage they afforded—and that the Monarch's bitter 'taste' was also 'beautiful' insofar as it protected it thus from the interest of possible predators. Another species of butterfly, in fact, mimics the Monarch's color pattern for this very reason. It may be late in the day to invoke such utilitarian concerns, but I wonder, finally, if we've ever truly had done with them. Certainly I hope not. Put simply, I want to know something—I want to know how and why and what it is, to be human—and I believe, as did Konrad Lorenz, that the arts give any of us the most specific, intensive information of those questions possible in the given world. If Kitaj were only a 'genius' insofar as painting was concerned—if he could not otherwise count beyond five or read a newspaper with a literate comprehension—delight me he well might, but it would be as the wind in the evening or the water's deep present blue. *I* am human, and I am restless, unsure, insistently questioning as to how *you* are feeling, what it is *you* know, and what do *they* mean. In Kitaj's art there is such a driven amplitude of attention, so many articulate layers of information and care. The axes of possible directions at times seem infinite—as if one might 'go anywhere'—and yet the preoccupation seems to me always rooted in the fact of the human: the singular, the communal, the one, the many, in the places of its history, in the presence of our lives. As he says, "No one can promise that a love of mankind will promote a great art but the need feels saintly and new and somehow poetic to me and we shall see. . . ." Here I believe that we do.

Three Films

Notes

for Gary Doberman

My layman's sense of this art finds a diversity of connections. Most generally, the nostalgic fact of first permission
to be 'entertained' or, more truly, to see *things* which otherwise could not be felt as 'real.' Hence—as with Jack Kerouac's lovely evocations of Saturday childhood afternoons
in wonder of local movie house—it was that miraculous 'outside' coming into one's sight, scrunched down in seat,
stuffed with popcorn, kids again in that insistent impulse of,
"what's going to happen *now*?" I think of how peculiarly
rare is that occasion, in a common life, when "the house
lights dim" and there is no question of the legitimacy of
specific anticipation, no judgment other than one's *pleasure.*

An art, any art, would seem to me to have to be *interesting,* so to speak. And what, among other things, would
seem so is that fact of a revelation, that an *information* occur—again, that *something happen.*

I've never felt that the arts had to be taken care of,
in some charitable way, and I've loathed the often preten-
tious context of interest, primarily social, which used the
activity for a badge of its own taste and/or its authority.

Ezra Pound years ago made a very simple statement in contradiction: "Damn your taste! I want if possible to sharpen your perceptions, after which your taste can take care of itself . . ." We surely will not all have the same "taste" but the arts are not 'about' 'reality,' nor are they merely instances of possible social agreement. No doubt they all make manifest factors of specific social habit and history—and that is interesting. But for *me,* selfishly enough, they begin at the beginning, which is to say, they constitute physically real acts, things, and occur in the world as objects of that order, to find use, effect, as all else in possible human experience will or will not.

As a writer I have been endlessly fascinated by the apparent fact that words, language, constitute a particularly human creation. I don't at all mean that we each one 'made it up,' that is, thought of an apple and then searched around for the appropriate 'word.' As Wittgenstein suggests, it is very difficult to think of thinking apart from the functions of language. However obvious it is to remark it, a dog does not 'talk' in the same way that we humanly do. Its barks, yelps, whines, etc., are not demonstrably an abstraction of something 'out there' into something 'in here,' my head, call it, where *indefatigable, shoe string,* and *water* may all find *a place* with no immediate necessity to be *here* otherwise at all. Sigfried Gideon in his book, *The Eternal Present,* proposes early on that the arts have a significant initial relation to the human ability *to abstract* and therefore *to symbolize*—and that, humanly, this power has both its obvious wonders and, equally, its distortions and evils. He would point to a crisis thus gathering in the Renaissance and coming to culmination with Descartes' famous statement: "I think, therefore I am . . ." Many ways now active in thinking, feeling, proposing, *using* 'the world' can contest his assurance, and the ego, the castle of this proposition, has long since been made to yield.

But, you see, there was never a "castle," certainly not here, in this room—and though I might track it as "castel-

lum" or as some memory of King Arthur and his knights—
did he even have, to speak precisely, an actual *castle*—or
how shall we now realize this *thing* which will in turn help
us, apparently, to make actual "ego" . . . A metaphor?
Symbol? *A figure of speech*—which instantly I translate to
the shadowy formation of some charming body, tentatively,
shyly, approaching—"a fine figure of a woman"—which in
turn provokes instant memory of a crony's accounting of
Hardy's somewhat peculiar fascination with hangings, in this
case of a woman: "She was a fine figure of a woman,
against the morning sky . . ." Death invites, day invites—
which D shall we follow?

Because—which word itself is only, dearly, *language*
"because" there is no 'because' other than in mind—it
seemed to me (and *seem* is the passive form of *see*) that *we,*
which is to say, no longer only *I*, had been wandering in a
seeming field of flowering possibilities which words precisely *make* actual to human attention and delight.

So my pleasure, as an artist, has had an abiding interest in that fact. Louis Zukofsky—extraordinary poet of our
mutual lives in the habits of the English-speaking world—
picked up Wittgenstein's: "A point in space is a place for an
argument . . ." But do I quote either correctly? Is it possible to make an 'incorrect' statement, or is virtue, forever
and ever, its own irreducible reward? That is, in language,
what *is* said is always the case—at least, for *what* is said, if
not for what is *not.*

But sitting again in the Maynard, Mass. movie house—
the Colonial, as I recall, as opposed to the People's Theater
—we are waiting for the movie to begin, presumably a western, and are we to think of it as a 'future' which will or
won't be 'correct'? I emphasize this aspect of 'correctness'
for many reasons—some personal, e.g., I dislike intensely
right people who tell me I am wrong; some rather shabbily
philosophic—"is this for real?"—and some quasi-scientific—
I would like to know if there might be ultimately a *correct*
way of living in the world, etc., etc. In poetry there has

been, I think, a marked respect for Coleridge's having called for "a willing suspension of disbelief." Shakespeare well before that—and I am sure many, many others in parallel situation—had asked that of his audiences, simply to admit the power of human gesture and language to transform an otherwise crunky approximation of the coast of Bohemia to affective, actualizing 'reality.'

I don't see—my thinking has so occluded my sight—how I'm now to enjoy anything at all in this situation. The movie seems hours in beginning, preoccupations proliferate and I'm again literally in this room, which is not 'this one' but another where I sit writing these words. Behind me, flat on a small cabinet-table, there is the severed muzzle of a literal bear's head, with intensely affecting eyes, although they are not 'real,' whose patience in that situation provokes and touches me. Where is the rest of his sad body? What was his life? He is a mute 'speaking' head no longer in time but as object—a whole world somehow attendant but never to be entered except by speculation: when was he otherwise? Where.

In some grotesque way, then, this part can manifestly stand for that whole—whether one means the 'all of it' or the gap, the space, the proposed 'rest of him' would imply. The interest for me here is in the fact that what's here can so clearly include all that apparently isn't. In fact, there is finally nothing else to be here at all, but what is here. One is amazed that, humanly, so much value can be given to what is absent as against what's present. Too, the root of that word, *absent*, would seem to be literally, *to be away*—which is presumably impossible, if one is anywhere at all.

Enough of this, so to speak. Clearly I like talking—I love the *places* words are, the things, the goings on, the mistakes and the accuracies. Writing is not, finally, some limited situation of dogmatic intentions. You must remember that film-making also wants to play, pun, echo, mistake, start over—and always is, at each point, only where it is, and all else that might be is there too. *Bear with me*, like they say.

Walking down streets daily, have you noticed that what's there is somehow true enough, i.e., it really seems to be there before anything else? I'd suppose that people who came upon the escaped hippo in that pond south of Los Angeles, assuming they knew nothing of its escape, would feel consternation, but its being there primarily would be their first impression one would think. Now if they didn't find it particularly interesting, to see such a thing, they are surely acting legitimately if they simply walk on by. But it doesn't seem so acceptable if they say, "why isn't it a giraffe, or the jolly Green Giant, or President Roosevelt?"

Film, as poetry, as the language arts more generally, is a serial art. One thing 'comes after' another: words, images. Often it's thought that artists in these mediums are extraordinarily conscious of specific intentions. No doubt some, even many, are. They have something to say. They think of the various possibilities open to them of saying it. They make resolution, and then they make the so-called art. Franz Kline said, "If I paint what I know, I bore myself. If I paint what you know, I bore you. Therefore I paint what I don't know." He isn't saying that he paints what he doesn't know *how* to paint—but that he paints what he cannot conceptually enclose as intention. *And* he is doing it with consummate intelligence of the possibilities inherent in such an 'open' situation—where what happens takes precedence over what 'should' happen—and with most alert perceptions. That's the point, for me at least, that the world be let in, that all the range of the art's powers of revelation, of doing something, be admitted. William Carlos Williams had a lovely qualification of the alternative: "Minds like beds, always made up . . ."

So—*one thing after another,* and what that factor has as powers . . . Have you ever played that game with others, where a piece of paper is folded, then one of the company begins a drawing, leaving a little bit of its line visible on another face of the fold adjacent, so that the next person continues the drawing with only those edges of line as a locus—

and so on, till the paper is exhausted? Then the paper is opened up to show the whole 'image'—and it is provocative because no one could anticipate what the image so con-structed would be. The congruence, rather the *contiguity* there used seems to me a very sturdy element in either film or poetry, and in human life as it is consciously experi-enced: "One day after another./ Perfect./ They all fit."

One would like to say, with respect to a poem, *read the words*—don't limit yourself to a preoccupation with what *isn't* being said. Again Pound is most useful: 'You can't blame a man for not doing what he isn't trying to do.' I tend always to take things literally, for whatever reason—that is, it took me some years to recognize that the name of a cafe in Santa Fe, LY 'N BRAGG, was not, specifically, the two names of its owners. So, in seeing anything, whether metaphorically or physically, I tend always to begin at that beginning of what it is that *is* there. Thus I'd want to say, look first, think later—and of course I want it to the ends of the world.

Williams—possibly in a somewhat defensive sense—said of a poem, that it was "a small or large machine made of words." The Abstract Expressionists insisted, with delight, that a painting was a "a two-dimensional surface covered (or not) with paint"—and presumably the factual, physical situation of a film is equally to be insisted upon. I know that Brakhage likes to remind us that a 'moving picture' is a sequence of rapidly changing single, static images. If pres-ently we are flooded with preoccupations of this kind, seemingly—I am thinking of the didactic, actually self-dramatic, insistence on process and its physical occasions—do recall that Brakhage is revealing the *means* of the film (much as Mélies asked Pathé to do), not the *ends* possible, which he has also so brilliantly shown us. I do believe, to say it, that life *is* its own reward—but I get absolutely ir-ritable if it has always to be a situation of, "look, Ma, I'm dancing!" I never did like dentists who explained what they were 'going to do' to me.

System . . . One time in college a friend, an Englishman, John Hunter, discovered a 'system' wherewith to win at the races. We all put in what we had, so that he could go to the racetrack in Providence, R.I., and win us a bundle. We put him on the train, and waited. Late that night comes a call from John, that he has indeed won—but in the celebration of that fact, has now spent all the money, etc. All these years later—I think my share would have been something like $78.27, not very much but surely *something*—that system really impresses me, and I finally had or have no argument with John's spending the money—but that's not the 'system' you understand. I mean, it's John, that pleasant, flush-faced sober-seeming bright English friend then, and that he *won*, you dig it? We *beat* the System! Terrific! Which is the only comment on structuralism I'd like to make at this time.

Personal . . . "and art is art because of you . . ." We are a *personal* so-called society, brothers and sisters. Don't get *personal* with me, was what she said. I think *persons* are some of the nicest people I know. "To tell what subsequently I saw and what heard . . ." Speak for yourself, John.

And so—to work!

1. *Western History*, Stan Brakhage

As Archie Moore once put it, via Melville, "The eyes are the gateway to the soul . . ." And another useful point, that Charles Olson was wont to emphasize, is that for primates the eyes constitute the most crucial sensory agency. What's called 'image,' then, means for us a most significant information, whether we consider it as an *interior* condition, that is, the *image* in the word *imagination,* or else the outside, those *images* we will momently see. If an imposition of necessary exterior 'meaning' anticipates our experience, clearly we'll see what we'll have of whatever necessity to see; for example, a driver's test will require us to see the forms of triangle, square, rectangle and circle as significant bits of information concerned with "stop," "caution," speed limit, etc. It would be impossible, I think, to discover anyone who did not have a habit of "seeing things" in particular patterns of received and/or habituated idea, as in "seeing red," for one instance. If the usual situation of literary narrative is then imposed on the activity of film, expectably the visual activity becomes a support of the story otherwise the case—as in a play or usual movie.

Brakhage tells a story without exception, but my point is that it is a story of visual information, not of literary details. In his earlier work, *Desistfilm,* for example, there was the grid of this other order, a narrative that might have been told in words. One might say that also of *Anticipation of Night*—but by this time the narrative is moving primarily as a visually defined activity, although the 'story' is still very clear in other possible terms.

As you see this film, you might think too of its title—although far better to put such preoccupations out of your mind. They are appropriately left to the occasion of afterthoughts in this case. But the film is, nonetheless, a particular experience of "history" and of "western history" in particular. Since this is not a test, you will not be expected to tell me or anyone else why.

You will certainly see many things that you'll recognize very simply. Colors, surely—forms, movements, even places and things. You'll be interested, I hope, by the *pace* of their interaction and by their divers contents more singularly. In short, you'll be seeing a specific rhythm of visual activity which is itself an obviously definite information. Much as in the case of poetry, these rhythms and the pace thus defined will have a very significant role. The parallel with constructs in music is useful also.

I remember asking Robert Duncan one time to identify for me all the ways in which *rhyme* might occur in poetry. So he rehearsed the familiar situation of sounds, e.g., full rhyme, *go blow*; assonantal rhyme, *get gain*; rhymes of rhythm, *until outside*; rhymes of parallel constructs, *in the box, up the hill*—and so on. Again you might consider how visual instances of rhyming are used here.

Finally, this is, simply, a *beautiful* film—which constitutes the possiblity of that literal pleasure I'd earlier spoken of. It delights the eyes with an intensive proposition of their very literal function: *to see.*

2. *Domicile,* Gary Doberman

Think of a couple of things, like they say: "Limits are what any of us are inside of . . ."; "Verse consists of a constant and a variant . . ." Already the world is here, truly, and anyone who has ever had experience of actual confinement—jail, hospital, body, army—common to human state can't really be patient with any assumption that we need to do it to ourselves. "The way out is via the door . . ."

Equally *measure* is a human preoccupation, even a responsibility, recalling Robert Duncan's "Responsibility is the ability to respond . . ." William Carlos Williams said in his humanly dear epic *Paterson,* "To measure is all we know . . ."

The artist has specific responsibility in that he or she is often in a territory of hitherto unacknowledged significance. As Pound put it, "Artists are the antennae of the race," and grand though that statement may seem to some of you, recall that artists in our present society have significantly made us aware of crises in our human world otherwise unattended. I am thinking, for example, of Allen Ginsberg's *Howl.*

In this film there is a simply accessible *constant* which you will have no difficulty in recognizing. There is an equally apparent *variable.* So your question—to phrase it poorly—might be, what is it that is being measured here? I know, intuitively and quite otherwise, that something, some factor, some common event, of human life is here manifest in a most literal way. Well, if you saw a person walking toward you, would you presume it to be a table? There is the circumstance, of course, when the inoffensive hatstand, in the dark, becomes the inexplicably malign monster. And the monster is as "real" as the hat rack. But first things first, so to speak—so consider, literally, again, what you are seeing.

The materials of this film are personal, comfortably so. Nothing in that way distorted or untoward. But the *choices* of the artist are both crucial and defining, and there is evident attention to what he has called *boundaries*. One is also impressed that there is such confident articulation of resources particular to film, marked technical skill—"without which nothing."

To contradict, in a way, what I've been thinking about here, I recall a friend of years ago, Tim Lafarge, who used to dance with Merce Cunningham. He told me at one point he used to work out by putting a dime on the floor of a closet, then getting in, locating himself on it, the dime, and seeing what bodily rhythms and articulations were then possible. So at various times and in various needs, there is great interest and use in devising the limits which increase perception of the resources also present nonetheless. "How to dance sitting down . . .", for example, which is my own preoccupation as I try to write these words—not at all metaphorically, because it *is* an absolutely physical event for me.

This too is a beautiful film, factually, with a lovely shifting counterpoint in the pacing. Like an old slow blues, after some up tempo number—so, read it and think.

3. *Short Films 1975*, Stan Brakhage

Being myself a very *personal* writer—which is to say, one who speaks always for himself despite the hopeful community I'd also insist upon in that fact—I'm dismayed, and often irritated, that the *personal* as a situation in experience of otherwise content comes now under attack. I grew up in a time which used to propose a kind of contest between the

objective and subjective. That should really date me for all
of you. Anyhow, people used to say things like, "let's take
an objective look at the facts" or, "you're getting too subjective." For the true scholars present, there's a piece I then
wrote called "A Note on the Objective," *Goad*, Summer
1951, collected in *A Quick Graph*—and I really haven't
changed a bit apparently in the twenty-seven years since. It
isn't that I love myself in some overbearing way, nor that I
think I have some privileged and authoritative information
of the world. But for me it *is* true that this complex piece
of meat, *me,* is factually the author of that 'world' the also
present 'I' has as experience. Did you know, for example,
that the word *world* comes from a root in *wiros* (Germanic),
which means "life or age of man . . ." I presume they left
the article out, because there never was "man" without one
or the other. Ok. So much for 'objectivity,' though a heavy
humanism would bore me equally.

But as Allen Ginsberg has it in "Wales Visitation":
"Particulars!" Or, Williams, "To tell what subsequently I
saw and what heard . . ." I am amazed that people can
think there is either information or record without the
agency of the human—that is, *for* humans, no matter what
the birds may be saying to one another otherwise.

So this last film is certainly *personal*, and I love it. I
take a lot of trips, I get stuck in drear motels, I dream of
home. There are two lovely instances of language in this
film which are really *right on*, like they say. Be it also said
the Brakhage is very aware of the powers of language, and
thank god he is *not* here tonight to hear me lay it on his
valuable creations. So—enough of that.

But—which is truly a great word, isn't it?—you know,
like, it never is the last word no matter what happens, death
included. But—don't we care what others feel in this life,
how they literally *have* a life? This film is so wisely, gracefully, *real* to that demand. I could never so actualize my
feelings in those places where these images were collected,
never substantiate those moments of true consternation,

yearning, witness, love as he does here.

"With your eyes alone/ with your eyes/ with your eyes . . . ," Ginsberg wrote in his never to be forgotten masterpiece, "Kaddish." Hear it. We are all related, we are all *here*. *See* this world we live in.

Placitas, N.M.
June 19-20, 1978

A Creeley Chronology
by Mary Novik

Robert White Creeley was born May 21, 1926 to Oscar
Slade Creeley and the former Genevieve Jules. Descended
from a family of Scots, Oscar Creeley was a well-known
physician with a practice in Watertown, Massachusetts. He
was head of Symmes Hospital in Arlington where his son
was born. A daughter Helen had been born four years previously. When Creeley was two his left eye was cut in an
accident and the eye was lost entirely three years later. His
father died when he was four and his mother, then in her
early forties, took up the support of the family by becoming the town nurse for Stow, then for the Actons. The family lived in West Acton on a farm not kept as such. Though
they later moved to a smaller place, Creeley had throughout
his childhood the freedom of fields and woods and learned
also New England habits of speech and behavior. He grew
up in his mother's family who were English and French
Canadians from Maine, and remembers his grandparents
very well.

Creeley was awarded a scholarship for Holderness
School, Plymouth, New Hampshire, in the Fall of 1940. He
stayed there three years and received an excellent and

kindly education. Articles and stories by Creeley appeared in the Fall 1940 issue of the Holderness news and literary magazine *The Dial* and continued appearing until the Summer 1943 issue. In 1942-43 he was Editor-in-Chief. He was also one of the editors of the school yearbook in his final year, and was the first editor of *The Holderness Bull* in 1943.

In 1943 Creeley was accepted into Harvard—had he gone to Amherst or the University of Pennsylvania, both of which offered him scholarships, he would have become a veterinarian—and disposed himself toward writing, although he did not commit himself until several years later. At Harvard he was taught by Gordon McCreary, F. O. Matthiessen, Harry Levin, Delmore Schwartz (creative writing), *et al.,* but it was in the friendships with Jacob Leed, John Hawkes, Mitchell Goodman (who married Denise Levertov in 1947), Slater Brown, Kenneth Koch, Seymour Lawrence, and many others that he discovered new senses of writing against the tradition of New Criticism and the social poetry of the thirties and forties. In 1944 he acquired a copy of *The Wedge* by William Carlos Williams and *Make It New* by Ezra Pound in 1946—both significant influences. (Pound, Williams, and the Objectivists surfaced as the mentors of a younger generation of writers in the late forties and early fifties.)

From late 1944 to late 1945 Creeley drove an ambulance for the American Field Service in the India-Burma Theater, then returned to Harvard via England. In his absence a group of friends had started the Harvard *Wake* as a protest against the *Advocate* and asked him to help edit the Cummings issue of Spring 1946, in which Creeley's first published poem, "Return," appeared. With other Harvard students he frequented the jazz clubs around Boston during the postwar years and spent much of his time listening to jazz at home. Creeley and Ann McKinnon were married in 1946 and moved shortly afterwards to Truro, Massachusetts. Commuting from there to Harvard and his lack of interest in several required courses caused Creeley to drop out in

1947, near the end of his final year. The Creeleys lived in Truro for about a year and a son David was born.

From 1948 to May 1951 the Creeleys lived at Rock Pool Farm, one-half mile east of Barrett's Crossing, near Littleton, New Hampshire. They were supported by the small income Ann received from a trust fund, supplemented by sustenance farming, though Creeley's main interest was in breeding pigeons and chickens which he exhibited in Boston shows. A son Thomas was born in December 1950. Creeley read a great deal of prose in those years and wrote much prose of his own, though only two stories, "The Unsuccessful Husband" and "In the Summer"—both written about 1948—have survived. In the Spring of 1948, *Wake* No. 6 appeared with two poems by Creeley and later that year *Wake* No. 7 with two more. The Summer and Autumn 1949 issues of another little magazine, *Accent,* each printed one poem.

In December 1949, Creeley heard Cid Corman's Boston radio program "This Is Poetry" for the first time and began an intensive correspondence with Corman which lasted until 1955. In January 1950 he gave his first public reading on Corman's program. (He read again on the program, and Corman read Creeley's stories on a third occasion.) In March and April 1950, Creeley broadcast five programs of his own, two on Williams, two on Joyce, on station WTWN, St. Johnsbury, Vermont.

In February 1950, disappointed in the magazines then coming out, Creeley decided to start his own with the help of a friend, Jacob Leed. He wrote to Williams, Pound (who provided many key contacts), and many other contemporary writers and editors, and gathered work by Williams, Charles Olson, Vincent Ferrini, Paul Blackburn, Paul Goodman, Samuel French Morse, Jacques Prevert, William Bronk, Cid Corman, Byron Vazakas, W. J. Smith, Donald Paquette, and Denise Levertov. The magazine fell through in July when they found it impossible to print on Leed's handpress. Within a month, Corman had decided to pick up the pieces for a new magazine of his own, to be called *Origin.*

On April 24, 1950, Creeley received his first letter from Charles Olson and from that date onward promoted Olson's work as actively as Olson promoted Creeley's own from his first reading of Creeley's stories. (From Spring 1950 to Fall 1951 Creeley wrote "The Lover," "The Seance," "Mr Blue," "The Party," "The Grace," and "Jardou.") Out of their correspondence in 1950 alone came the second half of Olson's "Projective Verse" essay (published in *Poetry, New York* in the Fall of 1950), Creeley's review of Olson's *Y & X*, Creeley's "Notes for a New Prose" and "A Note on the Objective," Olson's "Introduction to Robert Creeley," plus revised versions of Creeley's "Mr Blue" and "3 Fate Tales." Instructed by Olson's theories and poetry, Creeley struggled to find his own voice in poetry from Spring 1950 to Spring 1952. Meanwhile *Wake* No. 9 published three poems, and the Fall 1950 issue of *Gryphon* printed another.

In May 1951, the Creeleys moved to Fontrousse, near Aix-en-Provence, France, where they thought they could live more cheaply on Ann's income, though the atmosphere there and in nearby Lambesc, where they lived from May to October 1952, was discouraging. A daughter Charlotte was born in July 1952.

In the meantime, Creeley's (and Olson's) advice to Corman continued and *Origin* I, the Olson issue, appeared late in April 1951. It contained Creeley's first good poem, "Hart Crane," later reprinted as the first poem in *For Love,* his selection of poems written from 1950 to 1960. The Summer issue, *Origin* II, "Featuring Robert Creeley," was his first significant publication. It launched his writing career and secured his gratitude to Corman. (*Origin* II published four poems; three stories, "In the Summer," "3 Fate Tales" and "Mr Blue"; "Notes for a New Prose"; and excerpts from letters to Corman.) *Origin* I and II put the new writing movement on the road and provided the theory (Corman's essays on an oral poetry) and example (poems by Olson, Creeley, Levertov, *et al.*) for the new American poetry which was made generally accessible in 1960 by the publication of Donald Allen's milestone anthology, *The New American Poetry: 1945-1960*. The connection with Corman and the sympathetic outlet provided by *Origin* was a stimulus to Creeley second only to Olson from 1950 to 1955. Work by Creeley appeared in almost every issue of the twenty in *Origin*'s first series, from Spring 1951 to Winter 1957.

From 1950 to 1952 another useful connection for Creeley was with Richard Wirtz Emerson who with Frederick Eckman edited *Golden Goose* and published chapbooks of poetry. Three of Creeley's poems appeared in *Golden Goose*, Series 3, No. 1 (July 1951) and poems continued to appear in subsequent issues up to 1954. The Golden Goose Press published Creeley's first book, *Le Fou*, a book of twenty-three poems—nine of which were published simultaneously in *Golden Goose*, Series 4, No. 5—in October 1952. The poems had been written from 1950 to Spring 1952 and documented the process through which Creeley discovered his own poetic voice. *Le Fou* received notice in only one place, *Origin*, in an essay by Cid Corman in IX, Spring 1953.

After *Origin* II, though its effect was indirect (the first issues were far from sellouts), Creeley's work appeared regularly in avant-garde little magazines, a fact still true today, making it as difficult to locate his recent work in the seventies as it was in 1952. In the early fifties, Creeley's connections with these magazines were far less tenuous, in fact he was published largely by editors who admired his work. (Exceptions were John Crowe Ransom, who reluctantly accepted "The Unsuccessful Husband" and later "The Boat" for *Kenyon Review*, and James Laughlin, who found Creeley's stories "awfully dry and dull reading" but published a group of five, "Mr Blue," "The Seance," "The Lover," "3 Fate Tales," and "In the Summer," along with Olson's introduction, in *New Directions* No. 13 in December 1951. Steven Marcus spoke fairly of Creeley's prose while reviewing *New Directions* in *Commentary* in December 1952.)

Olson's friend Robert Payne of *Montevallo Review* published Creeley's *Y & X* review in the Summer 1951 issue, and Horace Schwartz published in *Goad,* from 1951 to 1952, two poems, a letter, and "A Note on the Objective." He also published the first attack on Creeley in print, a piece by Leslie Woolf Hedley in the Summer 1952 issue. In August 1951, a number of notes on storywriting were extracted from Creeley's letters by Katue Kitasono and printed with a picture (reversed) of Creeley in a beret in the Japanese magazine *Vou,* No. 35. Creeley's story "The Grace" appeared in the next issue, four poems in the two succeeding issues, and the essay "To Define" in Nos. 42-44 in November 1954. In the Summer of 1952 a poem appeared in the first issue of Vincent Ferrini's Gloucester magazine *Four Winds,* and Creeley's review of a novel by John Hawkes appeared in *New Mexico Quarterly.* The succeeding issue printed the story "Jardou," and a year later Creeley's review of Olson's *In Cold Hell, In Thicket* appeared. Since then a number of works by and about Creeley have been published in *New Mexico Quarterly.*

In January 1952, the first issue of Raymond Souster's Canadian magazine *Contact* appeared and Creeley was corresponding with Souster by the Summer. Six poems by Creeley were published before the final issue of March 1954, and three critical pieces ("A Note on Canadian Poetry," "A Note on Poetry," and a review of Williams' *Autobiography*) came out in *Contact* as well. In mid-1950, Creeley took on the job of American Editor for Rainer Gerhardt's German magazine *Fragmente,* though only two issues were published. (The second, late 1952, included translations of Creeley's stories "The Lover" and "The Seance.") Creeley was working on an American issue late in 1951 but it did not materialize.

In November 1952, on the advice of a young Englishman, Martin Seymour-Smith, who was tutoring Robert Graves' son William on the Spanish island of Mallorca, the Creeleys moved to Banyalbufar on the mountainous northwest coast of the island. (In October 1954 they moved to Bonanova, a town near Palma now overrun by the city.) The story of the breakdown of their marriage is told in Creeley's novel *The Island* (written Fall 1960 to Spring 1963) which collapses the events of the year 1953. The Artie of the book is Seymour-Smith who set up the Roebuck Press, with Creeley handling the American end, in the Fall of 1952. Disagreements over the quality of the books to be produced—Seymour-Smith wanted to economize on materials—caused Creeley to split off and form the Divers Press on his own. (Another point of dispute was Seymour-Smith's wish to publish Donald Hall, who had attacked Williams, Olson, and Creeley in *The World Review* in December 1952.)

Divers Press began by printing *Origin* VIII, which was Olson's *In Cold Hell, in Thicket,* in February 1953, then issued under its own imprint in June Paul Blackburn's *Proensa* and in July Creeley's second book, *The Kind of Act Of*—a book of sixteen poems written since Spring 1952. (Creeley's book was reviewed by Corman in *Poetry* in March 1954 and was mentioned by Louis Dudek in the Canadian magazine *CIV/n*, No. 5, in 1953 or 1954.) Books followed by Larry Eigner, Irving Layton, Katue Kitasono, H.P. Macklin (on pigeons), Seymour-Smith, Douglas Woolf, Blackburn's *The Dissolving Fabric*, and Olson's *Mayan Letters*, edited with a preface by Creeley. Divers Press also published Creeley's book of eleven stories, *The Gold Diggers* (which included three new stories written from 1953 to 1954, "The Boat," "The Gold Diggers," and "A Death") in March 1954, and an anonymous pamphlet of five new poems by Creeley, *A Snarling Garland of Xmas Verses,* as a gift for friends at Christmas, 1954. Ann Creeley, who had done much of the legwork, saw the last Divers Press book, Robert Duncan's *Caesar's Gate* (Duncan had come to Mallorca for a visit that Spring), through the press of Mossén Alcover in Palma in September 1955.

In the meantime, two anthologies which included work by Creeley had been published early in 1953: *Ferrini & Others* (Gloucester, Massachusetts: Vincent Ferrini) and *Nine American Poets,* edited by Robert Cooper (Liverpool: Heron). Creeley's third book, *The Immoral Proposition*—a book of eight new poems with seven drawings by René Laubiès—had been published by Jonathan Williams in Karlsruhe-Durlach, Germany, in the Fall of 1953. Creeley's connection with Canadian poetry was kept alive through contributions to *CIV/n,* and his correspondence with Irving Layton. Through Alexander Trocchi, he met a wild group of writers and editors who published *Merlin* from 1952 to 1955. (Cooper, Laubiès, and Trocchi appear in *The Island* as Willis, Lely, and Manus, respectively.)

By December 1953, the *Origin* poets had established themselves. An essay by Corman, along with the first French translations of poems by Creeley, Olson, Corman, and Levertov, appeared in *Le Journal des Poètes,* Brussels. Also in December, Charles Olson, in need of publicity for Black Mountain College, called on Creeley to edit *Black Mountain Review,* which was to become the most important little magazine of the fifties. The magazine scene had opened up considerably by 1953 and Creeley wanted an improvisational critical journal far different from the magazine he attempted to start in 1950 and equally from its result, *Origin.* The first issue appeared just before Creeley left Spain in March to teach at Black Mountain College. In July he took a leave of absence to return to his family. The Summer issue, then almost done, was followed in quick sucession by the Fall and Winter 1954 issues. Subsequently, three annuals for 1955, 1956, and 1957, were published. The reader should refer to Creeley's excellent introduction to the AMS reprint of *Black Mountain Review* [included here, pp. 16-28] and to the index published in *Serif,* II, ii (Kent State University Library, June 1965). Many of Creeley's own works, including a number signed Thomas White, Mauritius Estaban, R.C., W.C., and A.M. appeared in the seven issues.

From 1955, Creeley's poems began to appear in magazines he was no longer connected with, though most were still going into *Black Mountain Review* and *Origin,* or directly into his new books. His association with *Origin* was breaking down, and *Golden Goose, Fragmente, Contact, CIV/n,* and *Merlin* had all ceased publication. When Creeley left Spain in July 1955 to return to Black Mountain College, many other connections were severed as well, most importantly with his wife, Ann, and their three children. (Bob and Ann Creeley were divorced in 1955.) At Black Mountain College and in New York, Creeley's friendships could not fill the intensely-felt vacuum in his personal life, though wild episodes, of which there are equally wild stories, probably relieved the tension he was under. (Among friends of those years were Joel Oppenheimer, Fielding Dawson, Dan Rice, Jonathan Williams, John Chamberlain, Edward Dorn, Michael Rumaker, John Wieners, Louis Zukofsky, Edward Dahlberg, many of the New York Abstract Expressionist painters, and virtually all of the contributors to *Black Mountain Review.*) Late in 1955, Creeley's fourth book of poems, *All That Is Lovely in Men,* was published by Jonathan Williams in Asheville, North Carolina. It consisted of twenty-six new poems, a long preface, and fourteen drawings by Dan Rice, and received one review, by Frederick Eckman in *Poetry* in October 1956. (This review encouraged Creeley to submit more poems to *Poetry* though his work had been rejected several times previously.) *The Dress,* a book of poems and stories compiled in 1955, chronicled the break with Ann, especially in the stories written the previous Summer, "The Musicians," "The Suitor," and the title story. This book was in proof in 1957 but was never published.

Having resigned Black Mountain College subject to recall, Creeley set out early in 1956 for San Francisco (via Albuquerque, New Mexico), but really on a search for a new place to live and a new relationship. While in San Francisco, he gave a public reading and arranged for the printing of his fifth book of poems, *If You*—actually a portfolio consisting of eight new poems and four woodcuts by Fielding Dawson—by Henry Evans of the Porpoise Bookshop. (It was reviewed by Robert Beum in *Poetry* in September 1958.) While in San Francisco, Creeley met Ginsberg, Kerouac, Snyder, Whalen, McClure, Rexroth, Lamantia, Broughton, and Gleason, and gathered material for *Black Mountain Review* No. 7 (Fall 1957) which, with *Evergreen Review* No. 2, heralded the San Francisco "renaissance" in poetry. Though Creeley had begun to plan for No. 8, No. 7 was the last issue of *Black Mountain Review.* As he said, "whatever battle had been the case did seem effectually won."

Creeley returned to New Mexico in the Summer of 1956 and accepted a sudden opening in the Fall in a small day-school for boys in Albuquerque, teaching English, French, and later History, to grades 7 to 9. In January 1957, he met and within two weeks married Bobbie Louise Hoeck, thus acquiring two new daughters, Kirsten and Leslie. This and the teaching job provided a "security" which he had lacked for some time and the tone of his poetry began to change accordingly. *The Whip,* thirty-eight poems selected from his earlier books, was published that Summer by Migrant Books in Worcester, England, though the edition was bought out and sold in the U.S. by Jonathan Williams. (It was the first book to receive a number of reviews—at least four, one in *Poetry* in May 1958 by Louis Zukofsky.) Significantly, Creeley's first poem appeared in *Poetry* in August 1957. Now much in need of a bonafide profession to support his new family, he began to work on an M.A. at the University of New Mexico (Olson had "given" him a B.A. from Black Mountain College), taking three courses that Summer, and two at night while teaching Latin at the boys school for another year. A daughter, Sarah, was born November 17, 1957. In 1957 and 1958 poems appeared in *Hearse, Measure, Texas Quarterly, Evergreen Review,* and *Neon,* and reviews by Creeley in *New Mexico Quarterly* and *Poetry.* Frederick Eckman commented on Creeley in

Cobras and Cockle Shells (Flushing, N.Y.: Felix Stefanile/
Sparrow Magazine), and M.L. Rosenthal did the same in his
article in *The Nation,* November 1, 1958.

In the Fall of 1958, after a summer with his family in
Mexico, Creeley returned to teach one more year at the
boys school in Albuquerque. From 1959 to 1962, he acted
as contributing editor for *Inscape,* an Albuquerque newslet-
ter of poetry. On February 6, 1959 another daughter, Kath-
erine Williams (after William Carlos), was born. In April, an
impressive group of eight poems appeared in *Poetry.* By
July Creeley had handed in his M.A. thesis, a collection of
poems, to the University of New Mexico (he received his
degree the following year), and headed to California where
he read at San Francisco State on July 16 at the instigation
of Robert Duncan. In 1959 the first essay on Creeley, by
Robert Bly, appeared in *The Fifties.* Work by Creeley appeared in *A New Folder,* edited by Daisy Aldan (N.Y.: Folder Editions) and in a large number of new magazines, including *Yūgen, Big Table,* and *The Nation,* with few of
which he had any connection. From about 1959 onward
his custom was to send out what poems, if any, he had on
hand when asked for contributions, and in this way he has
appeared in an extraordinarily diverse group of magazines.
He also continued to write and publish critical prose regularly, as shown by *A Quick Graph: Collected Notes & Essays* (San Francisco: Four Seasons, 1970).

The Creeleys moved in the Fall of 1959 to San Ger-
onimo Miramar, Patalul, Such., Guatemala, where Creeley
tutored the five children of the *finca* owners plus Kirsten
and Leslie for the school year 1959-60. His sixth book of
poems, *A Form of Women,* in which his changed circumstances began to be reflected, was published in November
1959 by Jonathan Williams in association with Corinth
Books, New York. The book received seven reviews, in *Se-
wanee Review, Kulchur, Trace, New Mexico Quarterly,
National Review, Minnesota Review,* and *Sparrow. Four
Poems from "A Form of Woman"* was a booklet published

by the Eighth Street Bookshop in New York to celebrate the New Year, 1960.

In May 1960, ten new poems were published in *Poetry* (for which Creeley received their Levinson Prize) and he read for *Big Table* in Chicago. On May 29 the publication of Donald Allen's anthology *The New American Poetry: 1945-1960* opened the way for academic acceptance of Creeley and the other poets included. In 1960 as well, a poem by Creeley was published in *The Beat Scene,* edited by Elias Wilentz (N.Y.: Corinth) and seven stories appeared in *Short Story 3* (N.Y.: Scribner's). After 1960 (the year he was the D.H. Lawrence Fellow), Creeley's work was included in numerous books and anthologies published in the U.S., Canada, England, Germany, Sweden, Finland, Italy, Czechoslovakia, Argentina, and other countries. Creeley's poems have been included in every comprehensive anthology of contemporary poetry since 1960. A short essay on Creeley by John Fles came out in *Kulchur* in 1960, and an essay on Larkin and Creeley by Alan Brownjohn was published in *Migrant*—an English magazine which published much Creeley work from 1959 to 1960. As well, he was mentioned in an article in *TLS* September 9, 1960, and two significant works were dedicated to him: Olson's *Maximus Poems* (N.Y.: Jargon/Corinth) and Jack Spicer's mimeo'd *Homage to Creeley.* (From 1960 on there were an increasing number of dedications and imitations.)

In the Fall of 1960, the Creeleys returned to Guatemala for a second year and Creeley began, on September 7, to write the novel *The Island*, finishing the first four chapters within the month. He also typed up a manuscript collection of poems written from 1950 to September 23, 1960, and sent it off to Scribner's with the title *For Love*. In November, he wrote two stories, his first since 1954. ("The Book" was published in *Evergreen Review* September-October 1961, but "The Conversation" has never been published.) On February 12, 1961, Kenneth Rexroth's article (mentioning Creeley) on the new poetry appeared in *New*

York Times Book Review. In May, David Ossman interviewed him for *The Sullen Art* (N.Y.: Corinth, 1963). This
was his first published interview. Since then, interviews with
Creeley have appeared in various periodicals and have now
been collected in *Contexts of Poetry: Interviews 1961-
1971* by Donald Allen (Bolinas, California: Four Seasons,
1973). On June 1, 1961, Creeley recorded his poems for
the Library of Congress.

For the school year 1961-62, Creeley was Visiting Lecturer in English at the University of New Mexico, Albuquerque, where his stepdaughter Leslie was killed in a land-
slide in October. Creeley, however, honored commitments
to read that month for Contact Poetry in Toronto and at
The Poetry Center in New York. That Fall and Winter he
had a radio program on the local Albuquerque station
KHFM on which he interviewed Ed Dorn, Fielding Dawson,
Max Finstein, Winfield Townley Scott, and Witter Bynner.
In January 1962, not having written any fictional prose
for over a year, he wrote four new chapters for *The Island.*
In February, he gave a Benefit Reading for Poets Press in
New York and read in Seattle and Vancouver. On April 9,
For Love: Poems 1950-1960 was published by Scribner's,
New York. It was a *selection* of poems. Those left out of
that volume were later published in *The Charm: Early and
Uncollected Poems* (San Francisco: Four Seasons, 1969).
For Love was reviewed in over thirty periodicals and count-
less newspapers and has been far and away the most popu-
lar of Creeley's books, selling over 47,000 copies to date.
For Love was chosen as one of the leading contenders for
the National Book Award for Poetry in 1962. From 1963
onward, Creeley received increasing notice in newspapers,
magazines, and books. A complete listing may be found in
Robert Creeley: An Inventory, 1945-1970 by Mary Novik
(Kent, Ohio: Kent State University Press/Montreal: McGill-
Queen's University Press, 1973).

In the Spring of 1962, Creeley attended the Conference
on World Affairs in Denver. After the Summer, which in-

cluded a visit with Olson in Gloucester and a trip to New York where he was given a contract for the novel by Scribner's, the Creeleys moved to Vancouver where he taught at the University of British Columbia, 1962-63. In the Fall he wrote the third section of *The Island* and during the Winter, the fourth section. From September 1960, when he began the novel, to January 1963 Creeley wrote few poems, only sixteen of which were published (eleven at the beginning of *Words* 1967).

In the Summer of 1963, the Creeleys returned to New Mexico—he read at the University in May—to live in Placitas, a small town in the foothills of the Rockies twenty miles north of Albuquerque. They returned to Vancouver for the Poetry Festival, from late July to early August, organized by Creeley and Warren Tallman, which included readings and lectures by Creeley, Ginsberg, Olson, Duncan, Levertov, Whalen, and Avison. Creeley taught at the University of New Mexico 1963-64. On September 13, 1963 *The Island* was published by Scribner's and the generous reviews pushed the sales of *For Love* as well. This fact and others combined to make 1964 a breakthrough year in terms of academic response, especially after Creeley read with Duncan and Levertov at the Guggenheim Museum in New York in April. This was followed by readings by Creeley at ten universities. The June 1964 issue of *Poetry* published thirteen new poems, for which Creeley won the Leviton-Blumenthal Prize.

Since 1964, Creeley has read at virtually every major university in the U.S. and Britain. He has also read in France, Germany, Italy, and Canada, and in the Spring of 1976 went on an extensive reading tour of Fiji, New Zealand, Australia, Singapore, the Philippines, Malaysia, Hong Kong, Japan, and Korea. He has participated in many conferences, including: Buffalo Arts Festival (April 1965), Berkeley Poetry Conference (Summer 1965), writers' workshops at Oregon and Aspen (Summer 1966), Contemporary Voices in the Arts tour (Spring 1967), World Poetry Conference in Montreal (1967), Central Washington State College symposium (Spring 1969), International Poetry Festival at the University of Texas, Beloit College Lecture in Modern Poetry (Summer 1970), Neuvième Biennale Internationale de Poèsie at Knokke-le-Zoute, Belgium (September 1970), Second Annual Writers' Conference at the College of Marin, Kentfield, California (October 1970), Spring Poetry Festival, University of Massachusetts, Amherst (April 1971), Thomas Jefferson College National Poetry Festival in Allendale, Michigan (July 1971), Milton S. Eisenhower Symposium, Johns Hopkins University (October 1972), Buffalo Conference on Autobiography, S.U.N.Y. at Buffalo (March 1973), International Festival of Poetry, University of Toronto (October 1975).

In addition, he participated in many anti-war readings in the 60s, and has been writer-in-residence at a number of colleges for short periods. He has read at institutes as diverse as: The Center for Religion and the Arts, San Francisco (1971), The first San Francisco Book Fair (December 1971), Church of St. John the Divine (September 1974), Library of Congress (November 1974), Naropa Institute, Boulder, Colorado (August 1976), Philadelphia Y Poetry Center (November 1977), and the Poetry Center of the YM-YWHA, New York City (December 1977). In September 1966 and October 1971 the National Education Television film *Poetry USA: Robert Creeley* was broadcast. Two records released in 1969 contain readings by Creeley: Volume III of Today's Poets and Volume XVI of The Spoken Arts Treasury of 100 Modern American Poets.

So many books, pamphlets, and broadsides by Creeley have been published since 1964 that it is possible to note only the most significant ones here. *Robert Creeley: An Inventory* gives detailed information on those works published up to 1970. The expanded edition of Creeley's stories was first published as *Mister Blue* in Germany in 1964, then in Britain by John Calder and in the U.S. by Scribner's as *The Gold Diggers,* both in 1965. Since then there have been

Dutch and Mexican editions. The British edition of *The Island* was published by John Calder in 1964 and the German translation, *Die Insel,* by Insel Verlag in 1965. Creeley's poems since *For Love* have been published as *Words* 1967 and *Pieces* 1969 by Scribner's. Both have sold over 20,000 copies. *A Day Book,* an improvisational prose diary, was published in a deluxe edition for £850 by Graphis/Berlin in 1972, and was reprinted, along with new poems, under the same title by Scribner's later the same year. *Selected Poems* (Scribner's, 1976) reprints poems selected from *For Love, The Charm, Words, Pieces,* and *A Day Book,* along with more recent poems. *The Charm,* a book of early and uncollected poems published by Four Seasons in 1969, was reprinted in England by Calder and Boyars in 1971. Calder and Boyars have also published Creeley's collected poems in two volumes: *Poems 1950-1965* (1966) and *The Finger: Poems 1966-1969* (1970). In addition, a selection of poems have been published in English and German in *Gedichte* (Frankfurt: Suhrkamp, 1967). Creeley's new poems may be found in the small Black Sparrow Press books illustrated by Bobbie Creeley (*St. Martin's* 1971, *Thirty Things* 1974, and *Away* 1976), and *Hello: A Journal, February 29-May 3, 1976* (New York: New Directions, 1978).

In 1966 Creeley's edition of *Selected Writings of Charles Olson* was published by New Directions in New York. He also edited, with Donald Allen, *New American Story* (New York: Grove, 1965), and *The New Writing in the U.S.A.* (Penguin, 1967). His selection of Whitman's poems appeared as *Whitman* in the Penguin "Poet to Poet" series in 1973. In 1970 Creeley's collected notes and essays were published as *A Quick Graph* by Four Seasons. A radio play *Listen,* broadcast in Germany in 1971 and produced in London in 1972, was published with monoprints by Bobbie Creeley by Black Sparrow Press in 1972. *Presences,* a prose text to accompany photographs of Marisol's sculptures, was published by Scribner's in 1976. *A Sense of Measure* (an abbreviated version of *A Quick Graph*) was published by Calder and Boyars in 1972, and *Mabel: A Story and Other Prose* (A Marion Boyars Book) followed it in 1976. *Mabel* reprinted the prose texts from *A Day Book* and *Presences,* along with a new work, "Mabel: A Story."

From 1963 to 1967 Creeley was officially Lecturer in English at the University of New Mexico, though he was on leave of absence during 1964-65 as a Guggenheim Fellow, during Spring 1966 on a Rockefeller Grant, and during 1966-67 as a visiting professor at the State University of New York at Buffalo. Since 1967 Creeley has been Professor of English at SUNYAB, though he took a leave of absence during 1968-69 to return to the University of New Mexico, during 1970-71 to teach at San Francisco State, and during 1971-72 on another Guggenheim. In the Fall of 1970 the Creeleys moved to Bolinas, California, where they lived in an active community of writers and artists. In 1976 Creeley separated from Bobbie, and returned to Placitas, New Mexico, with Buffalo as an alternate home when he is teaching. In 1977, he married Penelope Highton, and in 1978 was made Gray Professor of Poetry and Letters at the State University of New York at Buffalo.

MARY NOVIK
1973 / 1978

FOUR SEASONS BOOKS

Robert Creeley	*The Charm: Early & Uncollected Poems* *Contexts of Poetry: Interviews 1961-1971* *A Quick Graph: Collected Notes & Essays* *Was That a Real Poem & Other Essays*
Edward Dorn	*The Collected Poems, 1956-1974* *Interviews*
Drummond Hadley	*The Webbing*
Dale Herd	*Early Morning Wind & Other Stories*
Philip Lamantia	*The Blood of the Air* *Touch of the Marvelous*
Michael McClure	*Ghost Tantras*
Pamela Millward	*Mother, a Novel of the Revolution*

Charles Olson	*Additional Prose*
	Causal Mythology
	The Fiery Hunt & Other Plays
	Muthologos:
	    Collected Interviews & Lectures
	Poetry and Truth:
	    The Beloit Lectures & Poems
	Proprioception

David Schaff	*The Moon by Day*
Gary Snyder	*Riprap & Cold Mountain Poems* *Six Sections from Mountains and Rivers* *Without End, Plus One*
Charles Upton	*Time Raid*
Philip Whalen	*The Kindness of Strangers* *Off the Wall: Interviews* *Severance Pay*

Edward Conze (tr.)	*The Perfection of Wisdom in Eight* *Thousand Lines & Its Verse Summary*

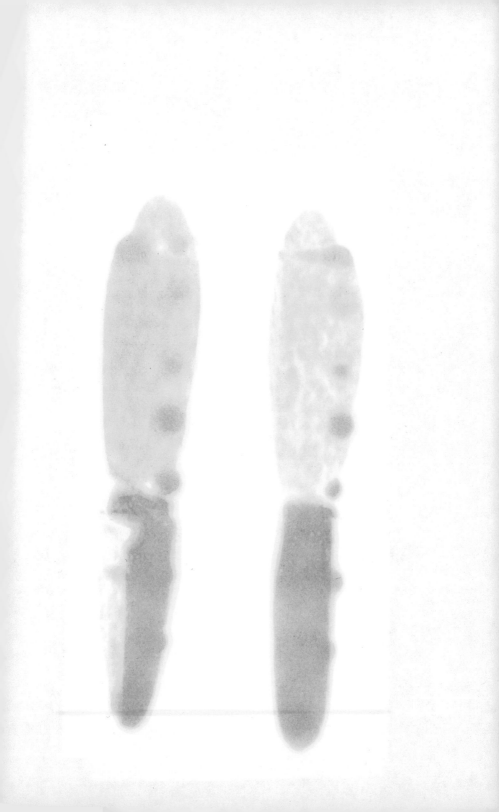

DATE DUE	